KB076692

아무나 못 만드는 토익책

발 행 | 2024년 07월 02일
저 자 | 구 원
펴낸이 | 한건희
펴낸곳 | 주식회사 부크크
출판사등록 | 2014.07.15.(제2014-16호)
주 소 | 서울특별시 금천구 가산디지털1로 119 SK트윈타워 A동 305호
전 화 | 1670-8316
이메일 | info@bookk.co.kr

ISBN | 979-11-410-9250-4

머리말

누구세요?

안녕하세요. 24년 6월 기준, 구독자 약 2만명을 보유한 유튜브 "구해줘토익" 채널의 운영자 구원쌤입니다. 토익 강의로 20년, 그 중 강남 학원(영단기, 파고다) 현장 강의 경력이 무려 10년, 현재는 에듀윌에서 인강, Y사 문제/교재 제작을 진행하고 있습니다. 시나공 토익의 대표 저자로 토익 교재만 11권 이상 집필했습니다. 토익 시험은 총 66번 990점 만점을 받았고, 시험 직후 정답 해설 강의를 10년간 진행했습니다.

무슨 책인가요?

토익 RC 파트5 (파트6 문제도 일부 포함) 250문제로 구성된 대략 100페이지 분량의 책입니다. 모든 문제들은 묶음 해설 강의도 제공되고, 개별 문제들에 대해서는 정답, 해석, 어휘 정리, 무료 해설 강의 및 온라인상에서 문제 풀어 보기 및 실시간 정답률 확인 링크도 제공됩니다. 한편, 인쇄본에도 QR코드를 같이 제공하여 접근이 쉽게 만들었습니다. 제공된 250문제는 모두 구해줘토익 채널의 매일토익 쇼츠로 올라왔던 문제들을 모은 것인데, 정답률이 낮은 것에서 높은 순서대로 정리하고, 문제 유형별로 한 번 더 정리를 하였습니다.

왜 만들었어요?

구해줘토익 채널의 쇼츠 영상 '매일 토익'의 컨텐츠가 참 좋은데 쇼츠 영상이다 보니 한번 보고 지나치게 되는 경우가 많아 한번 제대로 정주행을 해보고자 하는 학생들이 많아졌습니다. 이것을 하나로 정리한 자료를 보고 싶다는 구독자들의 요청이 있었고, 종이 책 형태로 풀어봐야 공부가 될 것 같다는 의견이 압도적으로 많았기에 책으로 만들기로 결정했습니다. 본 책은 쇼츠로 올라온 300문제 중, 매일 10문제씩 한달 (25일)간 마무리할 수 있도록 총 250문제를 엮었습니다.

누가 보면 좋아요?

여기 실린 문제들은 주로 한 회 30문제중 2-5문제 출제되는 고난도/함정 문제 수준의 문제입니다. 고득점이 목표라면 많은 양의 양질의 문제를 풀어야 하는데, 적어도 최근 10년간 출제된 문제를 구하려면 저작권 때문에 공식적으로 구할 수도, 양이 많아 다 풀 수도 없을 것입니다. 본 채널의 문제들은 이러한 출제 포인트를 적용하여 출제된/출제될 내용으로 구성한 것이므로 이를 다 풀어본 효과를 낼 수 있습니다. (250문제 이므로 수년간의 모든 시험에 나온 함정/고난도 문제가 커버되며 하루 10문제씩 25일 분량으로 학습가능)

모든 문제들은 실시간으로 반영되는 정답률과 오답률이 링크로 제공되므로 문제가 자신에게만 어려웠던 것인지 모두에게 그랬던 것인지 확인할 수 있습니다. 토익 목표 점수가 700이하인 경우는 이 책이 적합하지 않을 수 있습니다. 이 책은 분명 '명사 앞은 소유격이 답'이 되는 1초컷 문제는 거의 다루지 않습니다. 오히려 그렇게 알고 풀다 틀릴 수 있는 함정 문제를 다루고 있으므로 1초컷 문제를 먼저 학습하고 오길 추천합니다.

그렇다고 이것이 700점 이하의 학생들에게는 무의미한 책은 아닙니다. 1초컷 문제가 우선이긴 하지만 그 내용을 이미 다 학습했는데도 700점이 넘지 못했다면 이러한 문제를 통해 자신의 약점을 정복해야 하기 때문입니다. 본 책의 가장 큰 장점은 모든 문제들에 대해서 매우 간단한 방식으로 (유튜브 쇼츠) 무료 해설강의가 제공되므로 이해가 쉽고, 이미 많은 학생들이 남긴 댓글을 통해 추가적인 이해가 쉬우며, 궁금한 내용에 대해서 영상 아래에 바로 댓글을 달면 24시간 이내에 저자가 직접 답변해주므로 마치 1:1수업 같은 효과를 낼 수 있다는 것입니다.

책 사용법

1단계.
문제를 푼다

- 제한 시간에 맞추어 문제를 푼다. DAY01부터 시작한다. 교재의 문제들은 정답률이 낮은 것부터 높은 순으로 정렬되어 있기 때문에 만약 990점이 목표인데 현재 980점이라면 난이도가 높은 DAY25부터 역순으로 봐도 좋다.

제한시간 5분 / 틀린 문제 ___ 개
[10문제 해설] https://tinyurl.com/y72mcyf7

6. To meet our environmental goals, it is ------ that we reduce our carbon emissions.
(A) certain

2단계.
정답을 확인한다

- 문제 우측 상단의 QR코드를 찍어 링크로 들어가거나 pdf파일의 경우 링크를 클릭한다. 이때 연결되는 영상 모음이 있는 곳에서 정답을 확인한다. 휴대폰으로 접속했을 경우 '더보기' 부분을 누르면 더 쉽게 정답 확인이 가능하다.

3단계.
자기 것으로 만든다

- 강의를 들으면서 정답은 왜 정답이며, 오답은 왜 오답인지 이해한다.

- 자신이 틀린 문제만 확인하지 말고 맞힌 문제도 풀이법이 맞는지 확인한다.

해설

1. If our bodies don't get essential nutrients such as vitamins, they fail to perform their normal functions.

[해석] 우리 몸이 비타민과 같은 필수 영양소를 얻지 못하면 정상 기능을 수행하지 못한다.

[어휘] body 몸 essential 필수 nutrients 영양소 such as 예를 들어 vitamins 비타민 fail to ~하지 못하다 perform 수행하다 normal 정상 function 기능

[실시간 정답률] https://tinyurl.com/3axsk2zm
[해설] https://youtu.be/R_OqFlaKxck

- 각 문제 별 해석과 어휘를 확인한다. (교재 마지막 해석/어휘정리/해설 부분 확인)

- 각 문제에 대해서 최종적으로 해석이 가능하고, 정답뿐 아니라 오답에 대한 이유를 설명할 수 있는지 확인한다.

- 고득점이 목표라면 한글을 보고 영어로 바꿀 수 있는지도 확인한다.

- 이 과정 중에서 막히는 부분에 대해서 영상 아래에 질문 댓글을 단다. 문법, 어휘, 영작, 시험에 주로 나오는 내용, 같은 부류의 어휘 정리 등 무엇이든 질문 가능하다. 한글이 어려운 학생들은 영어로 질문을 남겨도 답변이 가능하다.

- 이미 비슷한 질문이나 그에 대한 답글이 있는 경우가 많으므로 한번 다른 질문 댓글/답글들을 보고 질문해도 좋다.

수행하다 normal 정상 function 기능↵
↵
[실시간 정답률] https://tinyurl.com/3axsk2zm↵
[해설] https://youtu.be/R_OqFlaKxck↵

구해줘토익
1년 전

다음시험에 나올 문제 입니다.
<구원샘의 매일 토익 #032> 해설은 요기:
https://www.youtube.com/shorts/R_OqFl
...
If our bodies don't get essential nutrients such as vitamins, they fail to perform their normal ------.

(A) functioned	0%
(B) functions	98%
(C) functional	0%
(D) functionally	2%

112명 투표

- 문제가 너무 어렵고 포기하고 싶다면 정답률/오답률을 확인하여 다른 학생들은 무엇을 선택하여 틀렸는지 확인한다. (교재 마지막 해석/어휘정리/해설 부분 확인)

4단계.
다시 문제를 푼다

- 3단계까지 해서 총 250문제를 다 마쳤다면 유형별 문제를 풀기 시작한다. 풀면서 예전에 풀었던 것이 막연히 답만 기억나는 것이 아니라 정답, 오답에 대한 해설과 해석, 어휘까지 완벽하게 기억나는지 확인한다.

목차

제 1 장

이것은 함정문제의 시작이다

DAY 01 정답률 98-92% 문제

제한시간 5분 / 틀린 문제 ___ 개
[10문제 해설] https://tinyurl.com/y72mcyf7

1. If our bodies don't get essential nutrients such as vitamins, they fail to perform their normal ------.
(A) functioned
(B) functions
(C) functional
(D) functionally

2. ------ the profits went up last year, there is room for more resources towards our research and development initiatives.
(A) Since
(B) Such as
(C) Due to
(D) Therefore

3. The owner of the restaurant is considering ------ free meals to the homeless during the holiday.
(A) thinking
(B) eating
(C) serving
(D) working

4. Munhwa Apparel's new line of men's suits is on sale this ------.
(A) cost
(B) store
(C) space
(D) week

5. Mr. Smith made a ------ guess at the population of the city.
(A) conservation
(B) conserved
(C) conservative
(D) conserve

6. To meet our environmental goals, it is ------ that we reduce our carbon emissions.
(A) certain
(B) reasonable
(C) important
(D) clever

7. We have yet to receive the report although a promise ------ that it will arrive by the end of the day.
(A) has made
(B) should make
(C) be made
(D) has been made

8. Zygo Corp made ------ updates to the Z-Car by incorporating a full-screen dashboard and facial recognition.
(A) irrelevant
(B) substantial
(C) talented
(D) trivial

9. We need an official permit at least one month ------ the start of the construction project.
(A) perhaps
(B) thanks to
(C) very
(D) ahead of

10. Rather than offer high-end equipment, the Downtown Gym keeps its membership fees ------ to those who work out every day.
(A) necessary
(B) optional
(C) active
(D) affordable

DAY 02 정답률 91-89% 문제

11. All employees are required to receive ------ from their immediate supervisor before using company vehicles.
(A) admission
(B) permit
(C) approval
(D) referral

12. The display cases in our stores makes our products ------ to customers.
(A) attractively
(B) attractive
(C) attraction
(D) attracts

13. The conference hall has a ------ of 500 people, making it ideal for large events and gatherings.
(A) vicinity
(B) capacity
(C) variety
(D) maximum

14. Due to ------ economic indicators, many businesses are reconsidering their expansion plans.
(A) weaken
(B) weakening
(C) weakens
(D) weakest

15. The Paradise Spa & Resort is now offering a 30-percent discount ------ repeat customers.
(A) by
(B) of
(C) on
(D) to

16. The newly designed helmet will ------ protect workers from head injuries.
(A) sooner
(B) stronger
(C) better
(D) faster

17. Mr. Frank praised the sales team for ------ securing a lucrative contract yesterday.
(A) frequently
(B) successfully
(C) surely
(D) generally

18. Maria headed to the pharmacy to ------ up her prescribed medicine.
(A) pick
(B) fill
(C) sign
(D) hold

19. Through these updates, users may no longer need to enter a password ------ prompted.
(A) when
(B) that
(C) how
(D) over

20. Mr. Norakai wasn't able to attend the seminar on May 1, ------ he was sick at the time.
(A) since
(B) when
(C) due to
(D) which

21. The blades of the fan should not be washed under running water. ------, delicately dust them off with a soft brush.
(A) In that case
(B) In the meantime
(C) Otherwise
(D) Instead

22. Due to the ongoing repaving work in the underground parking area, we kindly request your ------ and understanding.
(A) patience
(B) generosity
(C) payment
(D) punctuality

23. ------ there's a factory inspection scheduled for today, all product shipments will be delayed by one day this week.
(A) When
(B) As
(C) Whereas
(D) Unless

24. Having ------ the same wage for two years, Mr. Son was happy that his hard work had been recognized with a pay raise.
(A) received
(B) offered
(C) remained
(D) objected

25. Onsite childcare services among many perks at Apex Solutions are provided only ------ night shift workers.
(A) at
(B) for
(C) by
(D) with

26. The initiative ------ the community to monitor and report on climate change along the coastline.
(A) delights
(B) engages
(C) encourages
(D) appeals

27. Attached, please find my professional portfolio for your ------.
(A) explanation
(B) consideration
(C) attendance
(D) expectation

28. Chef Rivera opted to ------ dress the salad with olive oil and lemon for a fresh, zesty flavor.
(A) light
(B) lightly
(C) lighten
(D) lighting

29. Following the guidelines in MK Fashion magazine can make you look ------ in your professional outfits.
(A) stunned
(B) stunning
(C) stun
(D) stunningly

30. The morning meeting, at ------ they presented their quarterly results, was attended by top executives.
(A) time
(B) when
(C) which
(D) what

31. Our program offers training sessions ------ at young entrepreneurs to develop their business skills.
(A) targeted
(B) designed
(C) pointed
(D) thrown

32. Hunting activities are ------ to control by wildlife conservation agencies to ensure sustainable practices.
(A) subject
(B) forced
(C) delivered
(D) expected

33. BLK's laptop is sleek but ---- to use for intensive tasks.
(A) stylish
(B) heavy
(C) inadequate
(D) portable

34. To ensure safety, please read the ------ protocols on our Web site before running the machinery.
(A) operated
(B) operates
(C) operate
(D) operation

35. The government decided to evacuate the houses ------ the mountain after the flood.
(A) besides
(B) among
(C) around
(D) above

36. ------ technological advances also comes the opportunity to streamline manual work.
(A) As long as
(B) Along with
(C) Just as
(D) When

37. A marketing expert was hired to help sales associates ------ their ideas to prospect customers.
(A) create
(B) listen
(C) promote
(D) excavate

38. Some of the appliances in hotels are simple and functional as they are designed for ------ rather than aesthetic purposes.
(A) durability
(B) proximity
(C) expansion
(D) attraction

39. Moonlight Deliveries intends to ------ the construction of a warehouse in Busan.
(A) move forward with
(B) come across as
(C) watch out for
(D) look down on

40. Mr. Brown ------ his ability to make insightful investments to techniques he learned from his father.
(A) stressed
(B) attributed
(C) exceeded
(D) thought

DAY 05 정답률 83-81% 문제

41. Mr. Bake wrote an article urging the government to increase ------ of the nation's manufacturing sector.
(A) supervision
(B) supervisors
(C) supervised
(D) supervises

42. During the meeting, the manager spoke more ------ than usual to maintain a calm atmosphere.
(A) soft
(B) softer
(C) softness
(D) softly

43. Thank you for joining our membership. ------, you will be the first to discover our exclusive content and offers. Expect to receive your detailed welcome message shortly.
(A) Now
(B) Afterward
(C) Then
(D) In the meantime

44. Please be advised that critics do not always agree with the ------ of Northeast News and Post or the general public.
(A) views
(B) comparisons
(C) differences
(D) options

45. In order to provide ------, the board of directors asked Mr. Gu to extend his stay as CEO.
(A) duration
(B) indifference
(C) continuity
(D) validity

46. Mr. Arroyo worked for more than a decade at the Easton Group ------ joining Sunflower Houseware Ltd.
(A) by
(B) while
(C) since
(D) before

47. Formerly a renowned pianist, Ms. Park ------ runs a bookstore.
(A) now
(B) rather
(C) quite
(D) still

48. Archaeologists excavate old tombs and study ------ historical meanings through various techniques.
(A) where
(B) who
(C) their
(D) these

49. Mr. Genistein had his car that stopped working ------ last night's heavy rain repaired.
(A) because
(B) notwithstanding
(C) during
(D) though

50. The dinner ------ will be distributed right after they are checked for errors.
(A) invitation
(B) invitations
(C) invited
(D) inviting

제 2 장

실수가 아니라 실력이다

DAY 06 81-79%

DAY 07 79-78%

DAY 08 77-75%

DAY 09 75-74%

DAY 10 73-72%

DAY 06 정답률 81-79% 문제

제한시간 5분 / 틀린 문제 ___ 개
[10문제 해설] https://tinyurl.com/3ckp99r5

51. Artist Sebi MacDonad has been a ------ force behind the city revitalization project since its inception.
(A) sales
(B) motion
(C) creative
(D) gravity

52. Hearty Harvest ------ local stores in Seattle such as Harbor Grocers and Greenleaf Market.
(A) contracts
(B) supplies
(C) caters
(D) distributes

53. The electronic version of our latest report is ------ to the printed copy in terms of content and layout.
(A) better
(B) same
(C) equivalent
(D) convenient

54. ------ purchasing much fewer supplies, the Marketing Department spent most of its budget for the month.
(A) Upon
(B) By
(C) Despite
(D) Instead of

55. The Oasis Video Book proved to be a very good ------ to Grape's N-pad Pro.
(A) device
(B) choice
(C) option
(D) alternative

56. To keep productivity stable, the personnel manager should always attend to ------ department needs more employees.
(A) any
(B) whichever
(C) his
(D) that

57. Ms. Smith mentioned that the conference's complimentary breakfast was one appealing feature, while the free parking was ------.
(A) primarily
(B) second
(C) another
(D) already

58. Thomas Insurance's new policy provides full ------ against accidental damage to phones.
(A) guarantee
(B) coverage
(C) warranty
(D) security

59. Company representatives receive compensation for attending the convention and are ------ for travel expenses.
(A) reimburse
(B) reimbursable
(C) reimbursing
(D) reimbursed

60. Renowned for his expertise, Dr. Smith consistently keeps pace with the latest ------ in his field.
(A) examples
(B) versions
(C) components
(D) developments

61. The Aqualab keeps its air conditions adequately ------ for controlled experiments.
(A) moist
(B) moistly
(C) moisten
(D) moistening

62. Yummy Foodland has ------ to respond to local charities' needs with annual profits.
(A) promptly
(B) pledged
(C) before
(D) due

63. ------ the main air-conditioning unit is fixed, workers are allowed to use their own cooling devices.
(A) Because
(B) Basically
(C) Perhaps
(D) Until

64. To show appreciation for your loyalty, we sent you a ------ for $200.
(A) receipt
(B) charge
(C) certificate
(D) bill

65. The launch of an online marketplace has made local sellers excited about the ------ of reaching a wider customer base.
(A) preference
(B) automation
(C) prospect
(D) outsourcing

66. ------ to be the next big breakthrough in technology, Intech's new product has attracted significant media attention.
(A) Believed
(B) Believing
(C) Believable
(D) Believably

67. ------, employees attend company-wide networking events and socialize with one another.
(A) At times
(B) All at once
(C) In a moment
(D) At one point

68. ------ the firm has hired many new workers every month for the past 2 years, there are no signs of it doing so this month.
(A) While
(B) When
(C) Since
(D) Unless

69. The library updated its collection, ------ to include more digital resources over traditional books.
(A) opting
(B) opted
(C) options
(D) optional

70. All ------ of the new art museum will be preceded by a short meeting with a guide.
(A) tour
(B) tours
(C) toured
(D) tourists

제한시간 5분 / 틀린 문제 ___ 개
[10문제 해설] https://tinyurl.com/59wj5sbx

71. The HR department will conduct a ------ on office sustainability measures at 2:00 next Monday.
(A) research
(B) seminar
(C) speaker
(D) podium

72. Ms. Taylor will chair the annual charity gala, over ------ the city council has granted her full organizational discretion.
(A) there
(B) whether
(C) what
(D) which

73. ------ we are unable to accommodate diners indoors, we seat them in our outdoor patio area.
(A) What
(B) That
(C) As if
(D) Whenever

74. Mr. Johnson's ------ and dedication to his work were widely praised by colleagues and industry leaders.
(A) professor
(B) professionalism
(C) professional
(D) profession

75. Mr. Jeon decided to work as an intern as it had the ------ to result in a full-time position.
(A) addition
(B) ambition
(C) ability
(D) potential

76. Since early checkouts ------ cancelations, full cancelations fees can be charged.
(A) consider
(B) to consider
(C) are considered
(D) have considered

77. The eagerly anticipated renovation of the city library was made ------ thanks to a private donation.
(A) clear
(B) possible
(C) available
(D) honorable

78. It is imperative that the company ------ essential supplies without further delay.
(A) procure
(B) procures
(C) had procured
(D) is procured

79. In Ms. Johnson's -------, the marketing coordinator is responsible for managing the campaign strategy.
(A) absence
(B) behalf
(C) vacation
(D) duty

80. Tomorrow, our team will gather for the second time ------ the start of the new project.
(A) until
(B) since
(C) under
(D) along

81. We do not refund any damages caused by misuse, improper handling, or ------ user carelessness.
(A) else
(B) every
(C) other
(D) including

82. ------, the King Hotel could reach its full capacity, particularly when nationwide events take place.
(A) At times
(B) Previously
(C) Whenever
(D) Consistently

83. The developers document changes ------ the upcoming software update.
(A) of
(B) for
(C) to
(D) in

84. When the date for the annual shareholders' meeting -------, the organizing committee will send out the invitations.
(A) has been confirmed
(B) to be confirmed
(C) has confirmed
(D) is being confirmed

85. We are looking for experienced, ------ customer service representatives to handle inquiries during our peak business hours.
(A) several
(B) outgoing
(C) obvious
(D) respective

86. The International Association of Structures ------ the interests of architects all around the world.
(A) recreates
(B) represents
(C) delights
(D) shows

87. The lecture was delivered in a(n) ------ manner, making the complex topic both understandable and interesting to the audience.
(A) impersonal
(B) delighted
(C) engaging
(D) hectic

88. All outgoing products at SIM Tech are tested under ------ harsh conditions to ensure reliability.
(A) exactly
(B) deliberately
(C) anonymously
(D) extravagantly

89. The waitstaff at the restaurant greeted the guests with so much ------ that they felt invigorated.
(A) information
(B) feedback
(C) courtesy
(D) enthusiasm

90. ------ demand for sustainable packaging has prompted many companies to explore eco-friendly alternatives.
(A) Therefore
(B) Because
(C) Due to
(D) More

91. HY Industries engineers gave a facility tour to ten new recruits that were hired ------ the same day.
(A) as
(B) onto
(C) at
(D) on

92. It is not clear how ------ Adam Smith can be when he delivers a talk in front of large audience.
(A) persuade
(B) to persuade
(C) persuasively
(D) persuasive

93. The idea for the new marketing campaign ------ from a brainstorming session during the meeting.
(A) suggested
(B) approved
(C) originated
(D) delivered

94. Please have ------ four copies of the handout sent to the sales manager.
(A) as many
(B) other
(C) these
(D) several

95. Ms. Hedy's absence comes as ------ surprise, considering she has never been late for any meeting.
(A) something of a
(B) no
(C) little
(D) plenty

96. Employees who work remotely fear being forgotten ------ receive the same opportunities as those who don't.
(A) therefore
(B) but
(C) so
(D) nevertheless

97. Nordisk Industry's employees can be reimbursed for their tuition if they want to ------ a program in higher education.
(A) complete
(B) recognize
(C) adventure
(D) challenge

98. Kangaroos are indigenous to many regions of Australia but are ------ observed in residential neighborhoods.
(A) better
(B) almost
(C) commonly
(D) infrequently

99. Ms. Patel's ------ with her clients significantly increased her account retention rates.
(A) compliance
(B) proximity
(C) rapport
(D) understanding

100. We will talk about how we can increase a livestream's ------.
(A) view
(B) viewing
(C) viewer
(D) viewership

제 3 장
대충 알고 있으면 틀린다

DAY 11 72-71%

DAY 12 71-70%

DAY 13 69-68%

DAY 14 68-67%

DAY 15 67-65%

DAY 11 정답률 72-71% 문제

101. Fujiwara Automotive is committed to employee retention and ------ to management positions.
(A) chances
(B) alteration
(C) productivity
(D) advancement

102. Those ------ in the building received instructions to proceed to the nearest exit.
(A) remains
(B) remained
(C) remaining
(D) were remaining

103. Light meals are ------ delivered free of charge to office workers within the city limits.
(A) increasingly
(B) timely
(C) expressively
(D) typically

104. The organization's objectives and missions are summarized succinctly ------ its vision statement.
(A) on
(B) in
(C) about
(D) at

105. ------ two weeks, city work crews will collect green bins for such recyclables as glass bottles and aluminum cans.
(A) Every
(B) Only
(C) While
(D) Before

106. ------ all international school students are bilingual, and some of them can even speak three or more languages.
(A) Most
(B) The most
(C) Almost
(D) Mostly

107. If you don't have enough time to review the entire contract, please refer to a version ------ supporting documents.
(A) by
(B) without
(C) except
(D) in addition to

108. We are interested in knowing ------ the building's additions were to its facilities, including a new lounge.
(A) that
(B) who
(C) what
(D) which

109. Productivity in our office will stay consistent ------ many employees work remotely next week.
(A) though
(B) even if
(C) because
(D) so

110. Green energy usage is ------ across the globe even though many people still rely on fossil fuels.
(A) expand
(B) expands
(C) expanding
(D) expanded

DAY 12 정답률 71-70% 문제

제한시간 5분 / 틀린 문제 ___ 개
[10문제 해설] https://tinyurl.com/9amb5npr

111. According to the earnings projections, ------ things change, the Crown Company will fall behind its competitors.
(A) what
(B) which
(C) without
(D) unless

112. Kenshiro Motors's new compact model is well received because it has a spacious trunk without ------ interior space.
(A) enlarging
(B) sacrificing
(C) providing
(D) considering

113. Each salesperson on the team should ------ the results of his or her monthly sales.
(A) provide
(B) build
(C) reach
(D) appeal

114. The passengers waiting to board the train bound for Busan were informed that ------ would arrive 15 minutes late.
(A) they
(B) theirs
(C) them
(D) themselves

115. When the printer is jammed or ------ malfunctions, an error message will be displayed on the control panel.
(A) otherwise
(B) no longer
(C) in case
(D) whenever

116. Mr. Goodwill should take ------ look at the manuscript before submitting it to the publisher.
(A) more
(B) another
(C) much
(D) other

117. Health Vision will determine, based on the outcomes of the upcoming clinical trials, ------ the new drug can be moved to the next phase of development.
(A) if
(B) that
(C) as
(D) so that

118. Mr. Smith will oversee process ------ at the new facility in Chicago once the necessary team is assembled.
(A) innovate
(B) innovated
(C) innovation
(D) innovatively

119. As the business community has a great talent pool, ------ the HR manager picks will perform well.
(A) every
(B) some
(C) something
(D) anyone

120. As the ------ efficiently handled the implementation of the new policy, there was a notable increase in overall productivity.
(A) administers
(B) administration
(C) administrative
(D) administratively

제한시간 5분 / 틀린 문제 ___ 개
[10문제 해설] https://tinyurl.com/2cbmvxxf

121. Because of a pipe ------ in the lobby, the hotel shut down the area for the entire day.
(A) leak
(B) to leak
(C) leaked
(D) leaks

122. When addressing customer complaints, service representatives must offer solutions, within ------, to ensure satisfaction and maintain loyalty.
(A) reason
(B) role
(C) return
(D) range

123. Orion Technologies' revenue was sufficient to cover most ------ this quarter.
(A) expense
(B) expenses
(C) expensive
(D) expensively

124. Please note that organic greens must be cleaned ------ to ensure all residues are removed before they are eaten.
(A) freshly
(B) evenly
(C) lightly
(D) meticulously

125. ------ the one-day lecture Mr. Yang leads is very informative, it's the only one that provides role-playing activities and free consultations.
(A) Considering
(B) Because
(C) While
(D) Whereas

126. Fees in the local currency are subject to change ------ due to fluctuating exchange rates.
(A) monthly
(B) roughly
(C) overly
(D) properly

127. Alphacore Solutions, as a last ------, closed the branch after exhausting all other options.
(A) resort
(B) appeal
(C) minute
(D) day

128. All employees are encouraged to ------ any good ideas to make their work environmentally safe and friendly.
(A) contact
(B) persist
(C) think
(D) contribute

129. The Do More Unlimited plan ------ with free international calls to over 80 countries.
(A) provides
(B) coincides
(C) applies
(D) comes

130. Because of the high ------ of calls, customer requests may not be handled quickly during the peak season.
(A) order
(B) volume
(C) increase
(D) demand

제한시간 5분 / 틀린 문제 ___ 개
[10문제 해설] https://tinyurl.com/4bejffd4

131. Although the filmmaker ------- rejected Sam Anderson, his movie ended up winning an award.
(A) ever
(B) almost
(C) somewhat
(D) quite

132. Please ------ that the copier on the third floor is temporarily out of service.
(A) advise
(B) be advised
(C) advice
(D) advised

133. A book signing is one of the many events that are ------ in the course of the weeklong conference in Seoul.
(A) happening
(B) offering
(C) awaiting
(D) participating

134. The restaurant owner was delighted that the new menu ------ attract more customers.
(A) did
(B) caused
(C) made
(D) had

135. At the ceremony, Mr. Owen ------ a plaque in recognition of his contributions to the community.
(A) accepted
(B) congratulated
(C) awarded
(D) honored

136. Dr. Jones ------ introduced the guests who were scheduled to present at the conference.
(A) intuitively
(B) musically
(C) succinctly
(D) momentarily

137. ------ as a good speaker, Mr. Smith never fails to captivate with eloquence and charisma.
(A) Impressive
(B) Impressed
(C) Impress
(D) Impression

138. To better ----- our patients, our hospital offers a free reminder app with an easy-to-use calendar.
(A) serve
(B) care
(C) think
(D) function

139. The FAQ page on our Web site has ------ to the questions we get asked the most.
(A) answer
(B) answers
(C) answered
(D) answering

140. Mr. Kim will send the agenda ------ Friday's regular meeting before 5 o'clock today.
(A) by
(B) to
(C) for
(D) on

141. The lights went out just as the security guard ------ the area.
(A) has checked
(B) was checking
(C) checking
(D) had checked

142. Delightful Dining specializes in gourmet catering, ------ mass-produced, low-quality food options.
(A) rather
(B) but
(C) not
(D) except

143. Daisy's Diner, most of ------ dishes are enjoyed at its physical store, can be ordered online.
(A) whose
(B) its
(C) her
(D) that

144. Last year, the committee ----- an award as there was a need to honor community-helping businesses.
(A) notified
(B) initiated
(C) impressed
(D) created

145. The ------ of the road to a six-lane thoroughfare will ease the current traffic congestion in the area.
(A) widening
(B) widest
(C) widen
(D) width

146. Mr. Transkei filed a complaint form to the tech support team ------ a week ago.
(A) past
(B) over
(C) through
(D) within

147. Our president regards punctuality as a critical ------ for successful sales associates to possess.
(A) trait
(B) behavior
(C) action
(D) manner

148. The first salesperson ------ more than 100 contracts and receive the highest customer ratings will be honored at the awards ceremony.
(A) for securing
(B) secured
(C) to secure
(D) secure

149. The clean energy initiative was a success, ------ that the team's dedication and expertise were instrumental.
(A) prove
(B) proves
(C) proved
(D) proof

150. While most sales associates work in offices, ------ have the option to work remotely.
(A) which
(B) some
(C) other
(D) those

제 4 장

이 정도는 알아야 900 점

DAY 16 65-65%

DAY 17 64-64%

DAY 18 63-61%

DAY 19 61-58%

DAY 20 58-54%

151. The music event is offered free of charge, ------ beverages available for purchase from vending machines.
(A) because
(B) all
(C) and
(D) with

152. Due to enhanced efficiency measures, there will be ------ by all departments in energy consumption.
(A) reductions
(B) reducing
(C) reduced
(D) to reduce

153. If you need to buy a software package, select ------ integrates seamlessly with the existing system.
(A) the one
(B) whichever
(C) which
(D) any

154. At the conference, Ms. Williams announced ------ strategies Orion Dynamics will implement to improve customer engagement.
(A) single
(B) plenty
(C) that
(D) which

155. The board has approved a new policy ------ to streamlining operational processes and reducing costs.
(A) introduced
(B) permitted
(C) arranged
(D) dedicated

156. Ms. Shaniya recovered from her injuries just a few days ------ of her 26th birthday.
(A) before
(B) short
(C) because
(D) later

157. Using visual aids can help the audience ------ grasp the presentation's main points.
(A) well
(B) surely
(C) fully
(D) more

158. The local newspaper has an average daily ------ of 100,000 people in the region.
(A) reading
(B) reader
(C) readers
(D) readership

159. Our employees ------ that the company cafeteria provide a wide variety of food soon.
(A) expect
(B) express
(C) demand
(D) acknowledge

160. There is nothing at the ------ moment that the company can do to restore its reputation.
(A) suitable
(B) present
(C) this
(D) every

DAY 17 정답률 64-64% 문제

161. Our menu offers a wide range of options starting at ------ $5, so there's something for everyone to enjoy.
(A) last
(B) just
(C) least
(D) first

162. The Solomon Group has ------ Genova Innovation for an undisclosed amount.
(A) exceeded
(B) planned
(C) released
(D) acquired

163. According to the company regulation, all employees must ------ permission before attending external seminars.
(A) supply
(B) accept
(C) secure
(D) confess

164. The company had all earnings ------ destroyed due to the threat of regulations.
(A) estimation
(B) estimate
(C) estimates
(D) estimating

165. We've just appointed a new marketing assistant, and I am thrilled to have the opportunity to collaborate with ------ as skilled and dedicated as Ms. Sato. Let me introduce Mr. Son.
(A) her
(B) someone
(C) others
(D) him

166. The tour bus will ------ the national park, departing from the main gate every hour on the hour.
(A) spin
(B) rotate
(C) turn
(D) circle

167. Several flower arrangements ------ to the banquet hall before the awards ceremony later this afternoon.
(A) are being sent
(B) were sent
(C) will send
(D) had been sent

168. Many commuters find rush hour traffic simply ------ while trying to stay punctual.
(A) intolerant
(B) unbearable
(C) distracting
(D) cluttered

169. Ms. Jade's passion ------ others succeed has led her to the supporter program.
(A) that helps
(B) she helped
(C) for helping
(D) helping

170. Our hotel boasts 100 guest rooms, ------ with stunning ocean views.
(A) almost
(B) most
(C) mostly
(D) much

DAY 18 정답률 63-61% 문제

171. Subscribe to our premium luxury watch magazine ------ and receive one month of trial use.
(A) monthly
(B) always
(C) frequently
(D) today

172. With technology ------ rapidly, the company is investing heavily in research and development.
(A) advances
(B) advanced
(C) advancing
(D) advance

173. Mr. Han made complaints about the way many patients like ----- were treated in the hospital.
(A) himself
(B) those
(C) they
(D) them

174. Tech Innovations is making strategic changes to ------ with evolving industry standards.
(A) negotiate
(B) provide
(C) follow
(D) align

175. Those who live in rural areas are ------ in favor of building a hospital near their town.
(A) overwhelming
(B) overwhelmed
(C) overwhelmingly
(D) overwhelm

176. To ------ a maintenance request, report the issue with all relevant details through the online system.
(A) initiate
(B) propose
(C) recognize
(D) deliberate

177. The Premier Health Insurance package ------ with comprehensive dental and vision coverage.
(A) provides
(B) coincides
(C) applies
(D) comes

178. If you need support ------ regular business hours, our after-hours emergency service is available.
(A) beside
(B) during
(C) off
(D) outside

179. Debongi's Grocery clerks are trained to remain ------ to even the demanding needs of some customers.
(A) relevant
(B) prepared
(C) reliable
(D) attentive

180. The marketing team needs to ------ the target audience for our new product launch.
(A) decide
(B) determine
(C) appeal
(D) promote

DAY 19 정답률 61-58% 문제

제한시간 5분 / 틀린 문제 ___ 개
[10문제 해설] https://tinyurl.com/359wpmnz

181. The replaced laser printer ------ up to 30,000 pages per toner cartridge, requiring fewer replacements.
(A) looks
(B) limits
(C) produces
(D) uses

182. Café Delight's commitment to freshness is noticeable ------ its entire menu of artisanal coffees and homemade pastries.
(A) near
(B) between
(C) into
(D) across

183. All plants in the greenhouse are protected from ------, potentially damaging temperatures.
(A) high
(B) height
(C) highly
(D) heighten

184. ------ starting late, Ms. Park completed the task with an exceptionally impressive time.
(A) Rather
(B) Although
(C) Despite
(D) Nevertheless

185. Architect Kim is ------ with designing the innovative eco-friendly skyscraper in the city.
(A) credited
(B) capable
(C) agreed
(D) coincided

186. Ms. Uraha's new book explains ------ it takes to make one's hobby a successful business.
(A) about
(B) that
(C) which
(D) what

187. The magazine includes an article that ------ in detail how seriously global warming and air pollution can affect our lives.
(A) analyze
(B) analyzes
(C) analyzing
(D) is analyzed

188. ------ the grant proposal, the funding agency will evaluate its merits and decide on the allocation of resources.
(A) Having received
(B) To receive
(C) Being received
(D) What it received

189. The annual festival brings a burst of energy and excitement to every corner of ------ is otherwise a quiet town.
(A) what
(B) which
(C) there
(D) unless

190. If your order ------ any damage during shipment, we'll provide a replacement.
(A) causes
(B) sustains
(C) delivers
(D) occurs

191. The Riverdale Public Library will be closed for ------ three weeks during the renovation.
(A) several
(B) more
(C) both
(D) another

192. The stock price per share of Zenith Innovations is projected to ------ exceed $800 by the end of the month.
(A) exactly
(B) urgently
(C) relatively
(D) comfortably

193. Zenith Innovations has expanded its customer ------ in several new countries.
(A) basis
(B) bases
(C) based
(D) basing

194. The amount of money invested in the venture is ------ to be considerable enough to affect the local economy.
(A) seemed
(B) related
(C) deemed
(D) referred

195. Riverdale Electronics operates three branch ------ in the Greater Los Angeles area to better serve our regional clients.
(A) locate
(B) locating
(C) located
(D) locations

196. A ------ selection of genres at the city park's musical performance was offered compared to other concerts in the area.
(A) broaden
(B) broad
(C) broader
(D) broadly

197. The theater had to make program ------ due to the new performance schedule.
(A) adjusted
(B) adjusting
(C) adjustments
(D) adjustable

198. We will issue a new ID card that provides access to the laboratory as ------ your request.
(A) for
(B) per
(C) until
(D) upon

199. Seminar participants carefully ------ what others do in their group help finish collaborative work quickly.
(A) exam
(B) examine
(C) examining
(D) examinations

200. The members of the waitstaff were trained to serve additional ------ of side dishes only if they were requested.
(A) portions
(B) menus
(C) charges
(D) diners

제 5 장

만점이 목표라면

DAY 21 정답률 54-49% 문제

201. Launching the new product proved to be quite ------ for Electro Solutions.
(A) the experience
(B) experiencing
(C) experienced
(D) more experienced

202. We will inform you ------ design proposal we will select later this week.
(A) that
(B) this
(C) which
(D) whoever

203. This year's Literary Award will be awarded to Jonathan Parker, the lead author of the recently published novel 'Echoes of Eternity.' He ------ recognized during a ceremony at the Grand Theater on Sunday, May 5.
(A) was
(B) will have been
(C) is to be
(D) would be

204. Mr. Samson received an award for his creative ------ of new ideas into a business plan.
(A) submission
(B) configuration
(C) motivation
(D) incorporation

205. Mr. Park opted to pay for the furniture by ------ over a period of six months.
(A) installing
(B) installed
(C) installments
(D) installs

206. Honeyville and Pleasantville are becoming ------ of the fastest-growing towns in the province.
(A) every
(B) each
(C) both
(D) two

207. Employees at T&C cannot take more than one week of paid vacation ------ approval of the board of directors.
(A) unless
(B) except
(C) as a result of
(D) pending

208. After the concert, Ms. Smith searched for a limited-edition shirt, but there were ------ available.
(A) none
(B) nothing
(C) no
(D) not

209. A large amount of Chinese capital is being directed ------ acquiring a new entertainment venture.
(A) by
(B) since
(C) toward
(D) upon

210. Evergreen Hiking supplies the finest outdoor equipment and clothing ------.
(A) accordingly
(B) above
(C) around
(D) inside

DAY 22 정답률 49-41% 문제

211. ------ you opt to cancel your subscription, no further action is needed.
(A) In case
(B) Although
(C) Now that
(D) Even if

212. All sales are ------ during our clearance event, so choose wisely.
(A) final
(B) welcome
(C) discounted
(D) negotiable

213. The newly appointed project manager is ------ to feedback from her team members.
(A) open
(B) prepared
(C) available
(D) eager

214. Due to the construction work on 5th Avenue next week, there ------ minor delays.
(A) should be
(B) will have been
(C) has been
(D) to be

215. ------ the severe weather forecast, the company is implementing a remote working policy.
(A) Despite
(B) According to
(C) With regard to
(D) In light of

216. London Logistics ------ its incidental expenses by laying off its administrative workforce in addition to closing several local offices.
(A) to cut
(B) cuts
(C) is cut
(D) cut

217. Innovative technologies are enabling businesses to reach markets they might not ------ have accessed.
(A) near
(B) beforehand
(C) hardly
(D) otherwise

218. Zephyr Innovations will ------ its facility expansion to increase production capacity and meet growing demand.
(A) finance
(B) sponsor
(C) invest
(D) spend

219. No unauthorized personnel are allowed ------ to the secure data center.
(A) access
(B) to access
(C) accessible
(D) accessing

220. Providing feedback on a coworker could be uncomfortable, especially if there is ------ involved.
(A) critically
(B) criticism
(C) critical
(D) criticized

제한시간 5분 / 틀린 문제 ___ 개
[10문제 해설] https://tinyurl.com/mr22y7bp

221. Goldcable provides a direct withdrawal program that subscribers can apply ------ without complicated documentation.
(A) for
(B) to
(C) with
(C) at

222. One of our technicians will visit your facility to ------ the breakage that resulted from misuse.
(A) prevent
(B) cause
(C) support
(D) assess

223. Our menu features items from Lily's Confectionery, a ------ gem for years.
(A) neighbor's
(B) neighbor
(C) neighborhood
(D) neighborly

224. Farmers in Punjab offer fresh produce to local schools at a fraction of ------ prices.
(A) market
(B) reasonable
(C) reduced
(D) consisted

225. The product you ordered from our online shop is ------ until June 1.
(A) delivered
(B) valid
(C) unavailable
(D) postponed

226. Sales at Baxter Plaza ------ dropped when a rival superstore opened just a block away.
(A) urgently
(B) reportedly
(C) extremely
(D) properly

227. The new highway reduced the travel time from Los Angeles to San Francisco ------ 2 hours.
(A) by
(B) until
(C) within
(D) for

228. The manager is praised for being patient ------ her team members and customers alike.
(A) but
(B) to
(C) both
(D) with

229. Apply ------ to ensure all client communications are clear and detailed.
(A) diligence
(B) diligent
(C) diligently
(D) more diligent

230. Recognized as the trendsetter and industry standard, Oleo is the ------ domestic wine producer in the nation.
(A) indicative
(B) definitive
(C) supportive
(D) competitive

DAY 24 정답률 37-33% 문제

231. ------ a wide playground, the park will also feature a fully accessible multi-purpose field.
(A) Not only
(B) Beside
(C) On top of
(D) Furthermore

232. The promotional offer from Quick Deal Store is only ------ until the end of this week.
(A) heavy
(B) beneficial
(C) good
(D) limited

233. We didn't have enough time ------- the meeting to discuss the budget deficit.
(A) for
(B) to
(C) during
(D) except

234. The book *Ad Innovate*, ------ to be a key resource in digital advertising, has revolutionized modern marketing approaches.
(A) specialized
(B) seemed
(C) referred
(D) said

235. During our tour, we encountered a lot of traffic, which caused some delays. However, the highlight was our guide, who was excellent at bringing the history of each place to life with fascinating stories. The ------ thing I wanted was to rush through any of the stops without fully hearing the stories behind them.
(A) first
(B) important
(C) some
(D) last

236. Sebatonic Chemicals, Inc. announced today it has successfully developed a new variety of strawberries that ------ rising temperatures.
(A) resist
(B) resists
(C) resistance
(D) resisted

237. Many thanks to Rebecca Lin for the remarkable work on the Orion ------.
(A) accounting
(B) accounted
(C) accountant
(D) account

238. Ian Macdonald is among the top ten musicians in America, ------ only the Western Boys in album sales.
(A) towards
(B) except
(C) such as
(D) behind

239. The contractor was unhappy when the potential employer did not select ------ of the proposals.
(A) once
(B) anything
(C) which
(D) either

240. ------ the most popular structure in town, Sumatra Pagoda has been rarely visited in recent years.
(A) Once
(B) Aside
(C) Since
(D) Though

241. Mr. Wright wanted to ------ his coworker to some business opportunity.
(A) extend
(B) turn in
(C) alert
(D) inform

242. Celestial Movements is the fourth ------ broadcast documentary series in prime time.
(A) wider
(B) widest
(C) widely
(D) most widely

243. The renovation work will extend ------ Thursday if the weather becomes an issue.
(A) past
(B) above
(C) on
(D) at

244. Sal's Ristorante Italiano, ------ to be the most popular restaurant in town, provides authentic Italian cuisine.
(A) specialized
(B) seemed
(C) referred
(D) said

245. It's easy for you to purchase additional coverage ------ the manufacturer's warranty.
(A) in case of
(B) on top of
(C) as a result of
(D) including

246. Text Santonio Tech Support ------ immediate assistance with technical issues.
(A) to receive
(B) will receive
(C) receiving
(D) receive

247. With no laptops at their ------, most of the students in Peaceville were unable to attend online classes.
(A) use
(B) own
(C) disposal
(D) pace

248. Mr. Smith realized ------ he read the proposal it was a game-changer for his startup.
(A) what
(B) that
(C) whether
(D) the moment

249. The new product was completely sold out just a few hours ------ the morning.
(A) in
(B) into
(C) during
(D) of

250. The community center is ------ hosting a series of workshops on sustainable living.
(A) regularly
(B) recently
(C) formally
(D) timely

명사/형용사 자리 17 문제 (1/2)

1. If our bodies don't get essential nutrients such as vitamins, they fail to perform their normal ------.
(A) functioned
(B) functions
(C) functional
(D) functionally

5. Mr. Smith made a ------ guess at the population of the city.
(A) conservation
(B) conserved
(C) conservative
(D) conserve

12. The display cases in our stores makes our products ------ to customers.
(A) attractively
(B) attractive
(C) attraction
(D) attracts

14. Due to ------ economic indicators, many businesses are reconsidering their expansion plans.
(A) weaken
(B) weakening
(C) weakens
(D) weakest

61. The Aqualab keeps its air conditions adequately ------ for controlled experiments.
(A) moist
(B) moistly
(C) moisten
(D) moistening

90. ------ demand for sustainable packaging has prompted many companies to explore eco-friendly alternatives.
(A) Therefore
(B) Because
(C) Due to
(D) More

92. It is not clear how ------ Adam Smith can be when he delivers a talk in front of large audience.
(A) persuade
(B) to persuade
(C) persuasively
(D) persuasive

118. Mr. Smith will oversee process ------ at the new · facility in Chicago once the necessary team is assembled.
(A) innovate
(B) innovated
(C) innovation
(D) innovatively

149. The clean energy initiative was a success, ------ that the team's dedication and expertise were instrumental.
(A) prove
(B) proves
(C) proved
(D) proof

183. All plants in the greenhouse are protected from ------, potentially damaging temperatures.
(A) high
(B) height
(C) highly
(D) heighten

196. A ------ selection of genres at the city park's musical performance was offered compared to other concerts in the area.
(A) broaden
(B) broad
(C) broader
(D) broadly

197. The theater had to make program ------ due to the new performance schedule.
(A) adjusted
(B) adjusting
(C) adjustments
(D) adjustable

201. Launching the new product proved to be quite ------ for Electro Solutions.
(A) the experience
(B) experiencing
(C) experienced
(D) more experienced

219. No unauthorized personnel are allowed ------ to the secure data center.
(A) access
(B) to access
(C) accessible
(D) accessing

220. Providing feedback on a coworker could be uncomfortable, especially if there is ------ involved.
(A) critically
(B) criticism
(C) critical
(D) criticized

223. Our menu features items from Lily's Confectionery, a ------ gem for years.
(A) neighbor's
(B) neighbor
(C) neighborhood
(D) neighborly

224. Apply ------ to ensure all client communications are clear and detailed.
(A) diligence
(B) diligent
(C) diligently
(D) more diligent

동사/부사/전치사/접속사 자리 8문제

2. ------ the profits went up last year, there is room for more resources towards our research and development initiatives.
(A) Since
(B) Such as
(C) Due to
(D) Therefore

28. Chef Rivera opted to ------ dress the salad with olive oil and lemon for a fresh, zesty flavor.
(A) light
(B) lightly
(C) lighten
(D) lighting

42. During the meeting, the manager spoke more ------ than usual to maintain a calm atmosphere.
(A) soft
(B) softer
(C) softness
(D) softly

78. It is imperative that the company ------ essential supplies without further delay.
(A) procure
(B) procures
(C) had procured
(D) is procured

151. The music event is offered free of charge, ------ beverages available for purchase from vending machines.
(A) because
(B) all
(C) and
(D) with

175. Those who live in rural areas are ------ in favor of building a hospital near their town.
(A) overwhelming
(B) overwhelmed
(C) overwhelmingly
(D) overwhelm

184. ------ starting late, Ms. Park completed the task with an exceptionally impressive time.
(A) Rather
(B) Although
(C) Despite
(D) Nevertheless

199. Seminar participants carefully ------ what others do in their group help finish collaborative work quickly.
(A) exam
(B) examine
(C) examining
(D) examinations

7. We have yet to receive the report although a promise ------ that it will arrive by the end of the day.
(A) has made
(B) should make
(C) be made
(D) has been made

76. Since early checkouts ------ cancelations, full cancelations fees can be charged.
(A) consider
(B) to consider
(C) are considered
(D) have considered

84. When the date for the annual shareholders' meeting -------, the organizing committee will send out the invitations.
(A) has been confirmed
(B) to be confirmed
(C) has confirmed
(D) is being confirmed

132. Please ------ that the copier on the third floor is temporarily out of service.
(A) advise
(B) be advised
(C) advice
(D) advised

141. The lights went out just as the security guard ------ the area.
(A) has checked
(B) was checking
(C) checking
(D) had checked

167. Several flower arrangements ------ to the banquet hall before the awards ceremony later this afternoon.
(A) are being sent
(B) were sent
(C) will send
(D) had been sent

169. Ms. Jade's passion ------ others succeed has led her to the supporter program.
(A) that helps
(B) she helped
(C) for helping
(D) helping

187. The magazine includes an article that ------ in detail how seriously global warming and air pollution can affect our lives.
(A) analyze
(B) analyzes
(C) analyzing
(D) is analyzed

203. This year's Literary Award will be awarded to Jonathan Parker, the lead author of the recently published novel 'Echoes of Eternity.' He ------ recognized during a ceremony at the Grand Theater on Sunday, May 5.
(A) was
(B) will have been
(C) is to be
(D) would be

214. Due to the construction work on 5th Avenue next week, there ------ minor delays.
(A) should be
(B) will have been
(C) has been
(D) to be

216. London Logistics ------ its incidental expenses by laying off its administrative workforce in addition to closing several local offices.
(A) to cut
(B) cuts
(C) is cut
(D) cut

236. Sebatonic Chemicals, Inc. announced today it has successfully developed a new variety of strawberries that ------ rising temperatures.
(A) resist
(B) resists
(C) resistance
(D) resisted

유형별4
to부정사, 동명사, 분사 12문제 (1/2)

29. Following the guidelines in MK Fashion magazine can make you look ------ in your professional outfits.
(A) stunned
(B) stunning
(C) stun
(D) stunningly

59. Company representatives receive compensation for attending the convention and are ------ for travel expenses.
(A) reimburse
(B) reimbursable
(C) reimbursing
(D) reimbursed

66. ------ to be the next big breakthrough in technology, Intech's new product has attracted significant media attention.
(A) Believed
(B) Believing
(C) Believable
(D) Believably

69. The library updated its collection, ------ to include more digital resources over traditional books.
(A) opting
(B) opted
(C) options
(D) optional

102. Those ------ in the building received instructions to proceed to the nearest exit.
(A) remains
(B) remained
(C) remaining
(D) were remaining

110. Green energy usage is ------ across the globe even though many people still rely on fossil fuels.
(A) expand
(B) expands
(C) expanding
(D) expanded

137. ------ as a good speaker, Mr. Smith never fails to captivate with eloquence and charisma.
(A) Impressive
(B) Impressed
(C) Impress
(D) Impression

139. The FAQ page on our Web site has ------ to the questions we get asked the most.
(A) answer
(B) answers
(C) answered
(D) answering

148. The first salesperson ------ more than 100 contracts and receive the highest customer ratings will be honored at the awards ceremony.
(A) for securing
(B) secured
(C) to secure
(D) secure

172. With technology ------ rapidly, the company is investing heavily in research and development.
(A) advances
(B) advanced
(C) advancing
(D) advance

188. ------ the grant proposal, the funding agency will evaluate its merits and decide on the allocation of resources.
(A) Having received
(B) To receive
(C) Being received
(D) What it received

246. Text Santonio Tech Support ------ immediate assistance with technical issues.
(A) to receive
(B) will receive
(C) receiving
(D) receive

34. To ensure safety, please read the ------ protocols on our Web site before running the machinery.
(A) operated
(B) operates
(C) operate
(D) operation

41. Mr. Bake wrote an article urging the government to increase ------ of the nation's manufacturing sector.
(A) supervision
(B) supervisors
(C) supervised
(D) supervises

50. The dinner ------ will be distributed right after they are checked for errors.
(A) invitation
(B) invitations
(C) invited
(D) inviting

70. All ------ of the new art museum will be preceded by a short meeting with a guide.
(A) tour
(B) tours
(C) toured
(D) tourists

74. Mr. Johnson's ------ and dedication to his work were widely praised by colleagues and industry leaders.
(A) professor
(B) professionalism
(C) professional
(D) profession

100. We will talk about how we can increase a livestream's ------.
(A) view
(B) viewing
(C) viewer
(D) viewership

120. As the ------ efficiently handled the implementation of the new policy, there was a notable increase in overall productivity.
(A) administers
(B) administration
(C) administrative
(D) administratively

121. Because of a pipe ------ in the lobby, the hotel shut down the area for the entire day.
(A) leak
(B) to leak
(C) leaked
(D) leaks

123. Orion Technologies' revenue was sufficient to cover most ------ this quarter.
(A) expense
(B) expenses
(C) expensive
(D) expensively

145. The ------ of the road to a six-lane thoroughfare will ease the current traffic congestion in the area.
(A) widening
(B) widest
(C) widen
(D) width

152. Due to enhanced efficiency measures, there will be ------ by all departments in energy consumption.
(A) reductions
(B) reducing
(C) reduced
(D) to reduce

158. The local newspaper has an average daily ------ of 100,000 people in the region.
(A) reading
(B) reader
(C) readers
(D) readership

164. The company had all earnings ------ destroyed due to the threat of regulations.
(A) estimation
(B) estimate
(C) estimates
(D) estimating

193. Zenith Innovations has expanded its customer ------ in several new countries.
(A) basis
(B) bases
(C) based
(D) basing

195. Riverdale Electronics operates three branch ------ in the Greater Los Angeles area to better serve our regional clients.
(A) locate
(B) locating
(C) located
(D) locations

205. Mr. Park opted to pay for the furniture by ------ over a period of six months.
(A) installing
(B) installed
(C) installments
(D) installs

237. Many thanks to Rebecca Lin for the remarkable work on the Orion ------.
(A) accounting
(B) accounted
(C) accountant
(D) account

47. Formerly a renowned pianist, Ms. Park ------ runs a bookstore.
(A) now
(B) rather
(C) quite
(D) still

62. Yummy Foodland has ------ to respond to local charities' needs with annual profits.
(A) promptly
(B) pledged
(C) before
(D) due

82. ------, the King Hotel could reach its full capacity, particularly when nationwide events take place.
(A) At times
(B) Previously
(C) Whenever
(D) Consistently

105. ------ two weeks, city work crews will collect green bins for such recyclables as glass bottles and aluminum cans.
(A) Every
(B) Only
(C) While
(D) Before

106. ------ all international school students are bilingual, and some of them can even speak three or more languages.
(A) Most
(B) The most
(C) Almost
(D) Mostly

115. When the printer is jammed or ------ malfunctions, an error message will be displayed on the control panel.
(A) otherwise
(B) no longer
(C) in case
(D) whenever

131. Although the filmmaker ------- rejected Sam Anderson, his movie ended up winning an award.
(A) ever
(B) almost
(C) somewhat
(D) quite

156. Ms. Shaniya recovered from her injuries just a few days ------ of her 26th birthday.
(A) before
(B) short
(C) because
(D) later

157. Using visual aids can help the audience ------ grasp the presentation's main points.
(A) well
(B) surely
(C) fully
(D) more

161. Our menu offers a wide range of options starting at ------ $5, so there's something for everyone to enjoy.
(A) last
(B) just
(C) least
(D) first

170. Our hotel boasts 100 guest rooms, ------ with stunning ocean views.
(A) almost
(B) most
(C) mostly
(D) much

208. After the concert, Ms. Smith searched for a limited-edition shirt, but there were ------ available.
(A) none
(B) nothing
(C) no
(D) not

210. Evergreen Hiking supplies the finest outdoor equipment and clothing ------.
(A) accordingly
(B) above
(C) around
(D) inside

242. Celestial Movements is the fourth ------ broadcast documentary series in prime time.
(A) wider
(B) widest
(C) widely
(D) most widely

217. Innovative technologies are enabling businesses to reach markets they might not ------ have accessed.
(A) otherwise
(B) beforehand
(C) hardly
(D) near

240. ------ the most popular structure in town, Sumatra Pagoda has been rarely visited in recent years.
(A) Once
(B) Aside
(C) Since
(D) Though

48. Archaeologists excavate old tombs and study ------ historical meanings through various techniques.
(A) where
(B) who
(C) their
(D) these

57. Ms. Smith mentioned that the conference's complimentary breakfast was one appealing feature, while the free parking was ------.
(A) primarily
(B) second
(C) another
(D) already

81. We do not refund any damages caused by misuse, improper handling, or ------ user carelessness.
(A) else
(B) every
(C) other
(D) including

94. Please have ------ four copies of the handout sent to the sales manager.
(A) as many
(B) other
(C) these
(D) several

95. Ms. Hedy's absence comes as ------ surprise, considering she has never been late for any meeting.
(A) something of a
(B) no
(C) little
(D) plenty

114. The passengers waiting to board the train bound for Busan were informed that ------ would arrive 15 minutes late.
(A) they
(B) theirs
(C) them
(D) themselves

116. Mr. Goodwill should take ------ look at the manuscript before submitting it to the publisher.
(A) more
(B) another
(C) much
(D) other

119. As the business community has a great talent pool, ------ the HR manager picks will perform well.
(A) every
(B) some
(C) something
(D) anyone

150. While most sales associates work in offices, ------ have the option to work remotely.
(A) which
(B) some
(C) other
(D) those

165. We've just appointed a new marketing assistant, and I am thrilled to have the opportunity to collaborate with ------ as skilled and dedicated as Ms. Sato. Let me introduce Mr. Son.
(A) her
(B) someone
(C) others
(D) him

173. Mr. Han made complaints about the way many patients like ----- were treated in the hospital.
(A) himself
(B) those
(C) they
(D) them

191. The Riverdale Public Library will be closed for ------ three weeks during the renovation.
(A) several
(B) more
(C) both
(D) another

206. Honeyville and Pleasantville are becoming ------ of the fastest-growing towns in the province.
(A) every
(B) each
(C) both
(D) two

239. The contractor was unhappy when the potential employer did not select ------ of the proposals.
(A) once
(B) anything
(C) which
(D) either

19. Through these updates, users may no longer need to enter a password ------ prompted.
(A) when
(B) that
(C) how
(D) over

20. Mr. Norakai wasn't able to attend the seminar on May 1, ------ he was sick at the time.
(A) since
(B) when
(C) due to
(D) which

23. ------ there's a factory inspection scheduled for today, all product shipments will be delayed by one day this week.
(A) When
(B) As
(C) Whereas
(D) Unless

46. Mr. Arroyo worked for more than a decade at the Easton Group ------ joining Sunflower Houseware Ltd.
(A) by
(B) while
(C) since
(D) before

63. ------ the main air-conditioning unit is fixed, workers are allowed to use their own cooling devices.
(A) Because
(B) Basically
(C) Perhaps
(D) Until

168. ------ the firm has hired many new workers every month for the past 2 years, there are no signs of it doing so this month.
(A) While
(B) When
(C) Since
(D) Unless

73. ------ we are unable to accommodate diners indoors, we seat them in our outdoor patio area.
(A) What
(B) That
(C) As if
(D) Whenever

96. Employees who work remotely fear being forgotten ------ receive the same opportunities as those who don't.
(A) therefore
(B) but
(C) so
(D) nevertheless

109. Productivity in our office will stay consistent ------ many employees work remotely next week.
(A) though
(B) even if
(C) because
(D) so

111. According to the earnings projections, ------ things change, the Crown Company will fall behind its competitors.
(A) what
(B) which
(C) without
(D) unless

125. ------ the one-day lecture Mr. Yang leads is very informative, it's the only one that provides role-playing activities and free consultations.

(A) Considering

(B) Because

(C) While

(D) Whereas

142. Delightful Dining specializes in gourmet catering, ------ mass-produced, low-quality food options.

(A) rather

(B) but

(C) not

(D) except

211. ------ you opt to cancel your subscription, no further action is needed.

(A) In case

(B) Although

(C) Now that

(D) Even if

248. Mr. Smith realized ------ he read the proposal it was a game-changer for his startup.

(A) what

(B) that

(C) whether

(D) the moment

유형별9
명사절/형용사절 접속사 11 문제

30. The morning meeting, at ------ they presented their quarterly results, was attended by top executives.
(A) time
(B) when
(C) which
(D) what

56. To keep productivity stable, the personnel manager should always attend to ------ department needs more employees.
(A) any
(B) whichever
(C) his
(D) that

72. Ms. Taylor will chair the annual charity gala, over ------ the city council has granted her full organizational discretion.
(A) there
(B) whether
(C) what
(D) which

108. We are interested in knowing ------ the building's additions were to its facilities, including a new lounge.
(A) that
(B) who
(C) what
(D) which

117. Health Vision will determine, based on the outcomes of the upcoming clinical trials, ------ the new drug can be moved to the next phase of development.
(A) if
(B) that
(C) as
(D) so that

143. Daisy's Diner, most of ------ dishes are enjoyed at its physical store, can be ordered online.
(A) whose
(B) its
(C) her
(D) that

153. If you need to buy a software package, select ------ integrates seamlessly with the existing system.
(A) the one
(B) whichever
(C) which
(D) any

154. At the conference, Ms. Williams announced ------ strategies Orion Dynamics will implement to improve customer engagement.
(A) single
(B) plenty
(C) that
(D) which

186. Ms. Uraha's new book explains ------ it takes to make one's hobby a successful business.
(A) about
(B) that
(C) which
(D) what

189. The annual festival brings a burst of energy and excitement to every corner of ------ is otherwise a quiet town.
(A) what
(B) which
(C) there
(D) unless

202. We will inform you ------ design proposal we will select later this week.
(A) that
(B) this
(C) which
(D) whoever

9. We need an official permit at least one month -----
-- the start of the construction project.
(A) perhaps
(B) thanks to
(C) very
(D) ahead of

15. The Paradise Spa & Resort is now offering a 30-
percent discount ------ repeat customers.
(A) by
(B) of
(C) on
(D) to

25. Onsite childcare services among many perks at
Apex Solutions are provided only ------ night shift
workers.
(A) at
(B) for
(C) by
(D) with

35. The government decided to evacuate the houses
------ the mountain after the flood.
(A) besides
(B) among
(C) around
(D) above

36. ------ technological advances also comes the
opportunity to streamline manual work.
(A) As long as
(B) Along with
(C) Just as
(D) When

49. Mr. Genistein had his car that stopped working --
---- last night's heavy rain repaired.
(A) because
(B) notwithstanding
(C) during
(D) though

54. ------ purchasing much fewer supplies, the
Marketing Department spent most of its budget for
the month.
(A) Upon
(B) By
(C) Despite
(D) Instead of

80. Tomorrow, our team will gather for the second
time ------ the start of the new project.
(A) until
(B) since
(C) under
(D) along

83. The developers document changes ------ the
upcoming software update.
(A) of
(B) for
(C) to
(D) in

91. HY Industries engineers gave a facility tour to ten
new recruits that were hired ------ the same day.
(A) as
(B) onto
(C) at
(D) on

104. The organization's objectives and missions are summarized succinctly ------ its vision statement.
(A) on
(B) in
(C) about
(D) at

107. If you don't have enough time to review the entire contract, please refer to a version ------ supporting documents.
(A) by
(B) without
(C) except
(D) in addition to

140. Mr. Kim will send the agenda ------ Friday's regular meeting before 5 o'clock today.
(A) by
(B) to
(C) for
(D) on

146. Mr. Transkei filed a complaint form to the tech support team ------ a week ago.
(A) past
(B) over
(C) through
(D) within

178. If you need support ------ regular business hours, our after-hours emergency service is available.
(A) beside
(B) during
(C) off
(D) outside

182. Café Delight's commitment to freshness is noticeable ------ its entire menu of artisanal coffees and homemade pastries.
(A) near
(B) between
(C) into
(D) across

198. We will issue a new ID card that provides access to the laboratory as ------ your request.
(A) for
(B) per
(C) until
(D) upon

207. Employees at T&C cannot take more than one week of paid vacation ------ approval of the board of directors.
(A) unless
(B) except
(C) as a result of
(D) pending

209. A large amount of Chinese capital is being directed ------ acquiring a new entertainment venture.
(A) by
(B) since
(C) toward
(D) upon

215. ------ the severe weather forecast, the company is implementing a remote working policy.
(A) Despite
(B) According to
(C) With regard to
(D) In light of

221. Goldcable provides a direct withdrawal program that subscribers can apply ------ without complicated documentation.
(A) for
(B) to
(C) with
(C) at

227. The new highway reduced the travel time from Los Angeles to San Francisco ------ 2 hours.
(A) by
(B) until
(C) within
(D) for

228. The manager is praised for being patient ------ her team members and customers alike.
(A) but
(B) to
(C) both
(D) with

231. ------ a wide playground, the park will also feature a fully accessible multi-purpose field.
(A) Not only
(B) Beside
(C) On top of
(D) Furthermore

233. We didn't have enough time ------- the meeting to discuss the budget deficit.
(A) for
(B) to
(C) during
(D) except

238. Ian Macdonald is among the top ten musicians in America, ------ only the Western Boys in album sales.
(A) towards
(B) except
(C) such as
(D) behind

243. The renovation work will extend ------ Thursday if the weather becomes an issue.
(A) past
(B) above
(C) on
(D) at

245. It's easy for you to purchase additional coverage ------ the manufacturer's warranty.
(A) in case of
(B) on top of
(C) as a result of
(D) including

249. The new product was completely sold out just a few hours ------ the morning.
(A) in
(B) into
(C) during
(D) of

3. The owner of the restaurant is considering ------ free meals to the homeless during the holiday.
(A) thinking
(B) eating
(C) serving
(D) working

18. Maria headed to the pharmacy to ------ up her prescribed medicine.
(A) pick
(B) fill
(C) sign
(D) hold

24. Having ------ the same wage for two years, Mr. Son was happy that his hard work had been recognized with a pay raise.
(A) received
(B) offered
(C) remained
(D) objected

26. The initiative ------ the community to monitor and report on climate change along the coastline.
(A) delights
(B) engages
(C) encourages
(D) appeals

31. Our program offers training sessions ------ at young entrepreneurs to develop their business skills.
(A) targeted
(B) designed
(C) pointed
(D) thrown

37. A marketing expert was hired to help sales associates ------ their ideas to prospect customers.
(A) create
(B) listen
(C) promote
(D) excavate

39. Moonlight Deliveries intends to ------ the construction of a warehouse in Busan.
(A) move forward with
(B) come across as
(C) watch out for
(D) look down on

40. Mr. Brown ------ his ability to make insightful investments to techniques he learned from his father.
(A) stressed
(B) attributed
(C) exceeded
(D) thought

52. Hearty Harvest ------ local stores in Seattle such as Harbor Grocers and Greenleaf Market.
(A) contracts
(B) supplies
(C) caters
(D) distributes

86. The International Association of Structures ------ the interests of architects all around the world.
(A) recreates
(B) represents
(C) delights
(D) shows

93. The idea for the new marketing campaign ------ from a brainstorming session during the meeting.
(A) suggested
(B) approved
(C) originated
(D) delivered

97. Nordisk Industry's employees can be reimbursed for their tuition if they want to ------ a program in higher education.
(A) complete
(B) recognize
(C) adventure
(D) challenge

112. Kenshiro Motors's new compact model is well received because it has a spacious trunk without ------ interior space.
(A) enlarging
(B) sacrificing
(C) providing
(D) considering

113. Each salesperson on the team should ------ the results of his or her monthly sales.
(A) provide
(B) build
(C) reach
(D) appeal

128. All employees are encouraged to ------ any good ideas to make their work environments safe and friendly.
(A) contact
(B) persist
(C) think
(D) contribute

129. The Do More Unlimited plan ------ with free international calls to over 80 countries.
(A) provides
(B) coincides
(C) applies
(D) comes

133. A book signing is one of the many events that are ------ in the course of the weeklong conference in Seoul.
(A) happening
(B) offering
(C) awaiting
(D) participating

134. The restaurant owner was delighted that the new menu ------ attract more customers.
(A) did
(B) caused
(C) made
(D) had

135. At the ceremony, Mr. Owen ------ a plaque in recognition of his contributions to the community.
(A) accepted
(B) congratulated
(C) awarded
(D) honored

138. To better ----- our patients, our hospital offers a free reminder app with an easy-to-use calendar.
(A) serve
(B) care
(C) think
(D) function

144. Last year, the committee ----- an award as there was a need to honor community-helping businesses.
(A) notified
(B) initiated
(C) impressed
(D) created

155. The board has approved a new policy ------ to streamlining operational processes and reducing costs.
(A) introduced
(B) permitted
(C) arranged
(D) dedicated

159. Our employees ------ that the company cafeteria provide a wide variety of food soon.
(A) expect
(B) express
(C) demand
(D) acknowledge

162. The Solomon Group has ------ Genova Innovation for an undisclosed amount.
(A) exceeded
(B) planned
(C) released
(D) acquired

163. According to the company regulation, all employees must ------ permission before attending external seminars.
(A) supply
(B) accept
(C) secure
(D) confess

166. The tour bus will ------ the national park, departing from the main gate every hour on the hour.
(A) spin
(B) rotate
(C) turn
(D) circle

174. Tech Innovations is making strategic changes to ------ with evolving industry standards.
(A) negotiate
(B) provide
(C) follow
(D) align

176. To ------ a maintenance request, report the issue with all relevant details through the online system.
(A) initiate
(B) propose
(C) recognize
(D) deliberate

177. The Premier Health Insurance package ------ with comprehensive dental and vision coverage.
(A) provides
(B) coincides
(C) applies
(D) comes

180. The marketing team needs to ------ the target audience for our new product launch.
(A) decide
(B) determine
(C) appeal
(D) promote

181. The replaced laser printer ------ up to 30,000 pages per toner cartridge, requiring fewer replacements.
(A) looks
(B) limits
(C) produces
(D) uses

185. Architect Kim is ------ with designing the innovative eco-friendly skyscraper in the city.
(A) credited
(B) capable
(C) agreed
(D) coincided

190. If your order ------ any damage during shipment, we'll provide a replacement.
(A) causes
(B) sustains
(C) delivers
(D) occurs

218. Zephyr Innovations will ------ its facility expansion to increase production capacity and meet growing demand.
(A) finance
(B) sponsor
(C) invest
(D) spend

222. One of our technicians will visit your facility to ------ the breakage that resulted from misuse.
(A) prevent
(B) cause
(C) support
(D) assess

225. The product you ordered from our online shop is ------ until June 1.
(A) delivered
(B) valid
(C) unavailable
(D) postponed

234. The book *Ad Innovate*, ------ to be a key resource in digital advertising, has revolutionized modern marketing approaches.
(A) specialized
(B) seemed
(C) referred
(D) said

241. Mr. Wright wanted to ------ his coworker to some business opportunity.
(A) extend
(B) turn in
(C) alert
(D) inform

244. Sal's Ristorante Italiano, ------ to be the most popular restaurant in town, provides authentic Italian cuisine.
(A) specialized
(B) seemed
(C) referred
(D) said

16. The newly designed helmet will ------- protect workers from head injuries.
(A) sooner
(B) stronger
(C) better
(D) faster

17. Mr. Frank praised the sales team for ------ securing a lucrative contract yesterday.
(A) frequently
(B) successfully
(C) surely
(D) generally

21. The blades of the fan should not be washed under running water. ------, delicately dust them off with a soft brush.
(A) In that case
(B) In the meantime
(C) Otherwise
(D) Instead

43. Thank you for joining our membership. ------, you will be the first to discover our exclusive content and offers. Expect to receive your detailed welcome message shortly.
(A) Now
(B) Afterward
(C) Then
(D) In the meantime

67. ------, employees attend company-wide networking events and socialize with one another.
(A) At times
(B) All at once
(C) In a moment
(D) At one point

88. All outgoing products at SIM Tech are tested under ------ harsh conditions to ensure reliability.
(A) exactly
(B) deliberately
(C) anonymously
(D) extravagantly

98. Kangaroos are indigenous to many regions of Australia but are ------ observed in residential neighborhoods.
(A) better
(B) almost
(C) commonly
(D) infrequently

103. Light meals are ------ delivered free of charge to office workers within the city limits.
(A) increasingly
(B) timely
(C) expressively
(D) typically

124. Please note that organic greens must be cleaned ------ to ensure all residues are removed before they are eaten.
(A) freshly
(B) evenly
(C) lightly
(D) meticulously

126. Fees in the local currency are subject to change ------ due to fluctuating exchange rates.
(A) monthly
(B) roughly
(C) overly
(D) properly

136. Dr. Jones ------ introduced the guests who were scheduled to present at the conference.
(A) intuitively
(B) musically
(C) succinctly
(D) momentarily

171. Subscribe to our premium luxury watch magazine ------ and receive one month of trial use.
(A) monthly
(B) always
(C) frequently
(D) today

192. The stock price per share of Zenith Innovations is projected to ------ exceed $800 by the end of the month.
(A) exactly
(B) urgently
(C) relatively
(D) comfortably

226. Sales at Baxter Plaza ------ dropped when a rival superstore opened just a block away.
(A) urgently
(B) reportedly
(C) extremely
(D) properly

250. The community center is ------ hosting a series of workshops on sustainable living.
(A) regularly
(B) recently
(C) formally
(D) timely

4. Munhwa Apparel's new line of men's suits is on sale this ------.
(A) cost
(B) store
(C) space
(D) week

11. All employees are required to receive ------ from their immediate supervisor before using company vehicles.
(A) admission
(B) permit
(C) approval
(D) referral

13. The conference hall has a ------ of 500 people, making it ideal for large events and gatherings.
(A) vicinity
(B) capacity
(C) variety
(D) maximum

22. Due to the ongoing repaving work in the underground parking area, we kindly request your ------ and understanding.
(A) patience
(B) generosity
(C) payment
(D) punctuality

27. Attached, please find my professional portfolio for your ------.
(A) explanation
(B) consideration
(C) attendance
(D) expectation

38. Some of the appliances in hotels are simple and functional as they are designed for ------ rather than aesthetic purposes.
(A) durability
(B) proximity
(C) expansion
(D) attraction

44. Please be advised that critics do not always agree with the ------ of Northeast News and Post or the general public.
(A) views
(B) comparisons
(C) differences
(D) options

45. In order to provide ------, the board of directors asked Mr. Gu to extend his stay as CEO.
(A) duration
(B) indifference
(C) continuity
(D) validity

51. Artist Sebi MacDonad has been a ------ force behind the city revitalization project since its inception.
(A) sales
(B) motion
(C) creative
(D) gravity

55. The Oasis Video Book proved to be a very good ------ to Grape's N-pad Pro.
(A) device
(B) choice
(C) option
(D) alternative

58. Thomas Insurance's new policy provides full ------ against accidental damage to phones.
(A) guarantee
(B) coverage
(C) warranty
(D) security

60. Renowned for his expertise, Dr. Smith consistently keeps pace with the latest ------ in his field.
(A) examples
(B) versions
(C) components
(D) developments

64. To show appreciation for your loyalty, we sent you a ------ for $200.
(A) receipt
(B) charge
(C) certificate
(D) bill

65. The launch of an online marketplace has made local sellers excited about the ------ of reaching a wider customer base.
(A) preference
(B) automation
(C) prospect
(D) outsourcing

71. The HR department will conduct a ------ on office sustainability measures at 2:00 next Monday.
(A) research
(B) seminar
(C) speaker
(D) podium

75. Mr. Jeon decided to work as an intern as it had the ------ to result in a full-time position.
(A) addition
(B) ambition
(C) ability
(D) potential

79. In Ms. Johnson's -------, the marketing coordinator is responsible for managing the campaign strategy.
(A) absence
(B) behalf
(C) vacation
(D) duty

89. The waitstaff at the restaurant greeted the guests with so much ------ that they felt invigorated.
(A) information
(B) feedback
(C) courtesy
(D) enthusiasm

99. Ms. Patel's ------ with her clients significantly increased her account retention rates.
(A) compliance
(B) proximity
(C) rapport
(D) understanding

101. Fujiwara Automotive is committed to employee retention and ------ to management positions.
(A) chances
(B) alteration
(C) productivity
(D) advancement

122. When addressing customer complaints, service representatives must offer solutions, within ------, to ensure satisfaction and maintain loyalty.
(A) reason
(B) role
(C) return
(D) range

127. Alphacore Solutions, as a last ------, closed the branch after exhausting all other options.
(A) resort
(B) appeal
(C) minute
(D) day

130. Because of the high ------ of calls, customer requests may not be handled quickly during the peak season.
(A) order
(B) volume
(C) increase
(D) demand

147. Our president regards punctuality as a critical ------ for successful sales associates to possess.
(A) trait
(B) behavior
(C) action
(D) manner

200. The members of the waitstaff were trained to serve additional ------ of side dishes only if they were requested.
(A) portions
(B) menus
(C) charges
(D) diners

204. Mr. Samson received an award for his creative ------ of new ideas into a business plan.
(A) submission
(B) configuration
(C) motivation
(D) incorporation

247. With no laptops at their ------, most of the students in Peaceville were unable to attend online classes.
(A) use
(B) own
(C) disposal
(D) pace

6. To meet our environmental goals, it is ------ that we reduce our carbon emissions.
(A) certain
(B) reasonable
(C) important
(D) clever

8. Zygo Corp made ------ updates to the Z-Car by incorporating a full-screen dashboard and facial recognition.
(A) irrelevant
(B) substantial
(C) talented
(D) trivial

10. Rather than offer high-end equipment, the Downtown Gym keeps its membership fees ------ to those who work out every day.
(A) necessary
(B) optional
(C) active
(D) affordable

32. Hunting activities are ------ to control by wildlife conservation agencies to ensure sustainable practices.
(A) subject
(B) forced
(C) delivered
(D) expected

33. BLK's laptop is sleek but ---- to use for intensive tasks.
(A) stylish
(B) heavy
(C) inadequate
(D) portable

53. The electronic version of our latest report is ------ to the printed copy in terms of content and layout.
(A) better
(B) same
(C) equivalent
(D) convenient

77. The eagerly anticipated renovation of the city library was made ------ thanks to a private donation.
(A) clear
(B) possible
(C) available
(D) honorable

85. We are looking for experienced, ------ customer service representatives to handle inquiries during our peak business hours.
(A) several
(B) outgoing
(C) obvious
(D) respective

87. The lecture was delivered in a(n) ------ manner, making the complex topic both understandable and interesting to the audience.
(A) impersonal
(B) delighted
(C) engaging
(D) hectic

160. There is nothing at the ------ moment that the company can do to restore its reputation.
(A) suitable
(B) present
(C) this
(D) every

168. Many commuters find rush hour traffic simply ------ while trying to stay punctual.
(A) intolerant
(B) unbearable
(C) distracting
(D) cluttered

179. Debongi's Grocery clerks are trained to remain ------ to even the demanding needs of some customers.
(A) relevant
(B) prepared
(C) reliable
(D) attentive

194. The amount of money invested in the venture is ------ to be considerable enough to affect the local economy.
(A) seemed
(B) related
(C) deemed
(D) referred

212. All sales are ------ during our clearance event, so choose wisely.
(A) final
(B) welcome
(C) discounted
(D) negotiable

213. The newly appointed project manager is ------ to feedback from her team members.
(A) open
(B) prepared
(C) available
(D) eager

224. Farmers in Punjab offer fresh produce to local schools at a fraction of ------ prices.
(A) market
(B) reasonable
(C) reduced
(D) consisted

230. Recognized as the trendsetter and industry standard, Oleo is the ------ domestic wine producer in the nation.
(A) indicative
(B) definitive
(C) supportive
(D) competitive

232. The promotional offer from Quick Deal Store is only ------ until the end of this week.
(A) heavy
(B) beneficial
(C) good
(D) limited

235. During our tour, we encountered a lot of traffic, which caused some delays. However, the highlight was our guide, who was excellent at bringing the history of each place to life with fascinating stories. The ------ thing I wanted was to rush through any of the stops without fully hearing the stories behind them.
(A) first
(B) important
(C) some
(D) last

해설

1. If our bodies don't get essential nutrients such as vitamins, they fail to perform their normal functions.

[해석] 우리 몸이 비타민과 같은 필수 영양소를 얻지 못하면 정상 기능을 수행하지 못한다.

[어휘] body 몸 essential 필수 nutrients 영양소 such as 예를 들어 vitamins 비타민 fail to ~하지 못하다 perform 수행하다 normal 정상 function 기능

[실시간 정답률] https://tinyurl.com/3axsk2zm
[해설] https://youtu.be/R_OqFlaKxck

2. Since the profits went up last year, there is room for more resources towards our research and development initiatives.

[해석] 작년에 이익이 증가했기 때문에, 연구 및 개발 계획에 더 많은 자원을 할당할 여지가 있다.

[어휘] profit 이익 go up 증가하다 last year 작년 room 여지 resources 자원 research 연구 development 개발 initiatives 계획 since ~때문에

[실시간 정답률] https://tinyurl.com/dc2en6ww
[해설] https://youtu.be/uzfcZxj57cA

3. The owner of the restaurant is considering serving free meals to the homeless during the holiday.

[해석] 식당의 주인은 명절 동안 노숙자들에게 무료로 식사를 제공하는 것을 고려하고 있다.

[어휘] owner 주인 restaurant 식당 consider 고려하다 free meals 무료 식사 homeless 노숙자들 holiday 명절

[실시간 정답률] https://tinyurl.com/5hcxseu6
[해설] https://youtu.be/fGBxjqR7Duw

4. Munhwa Apparel's new line of men's suits is on sale this week.

[해석] 문화 의류의 새로운 남성 정장 라인은 이번 주에 할인 판매 중이다.

[어휘] new line 새로운 제품군 men's suits 남성 정장 on sale 할인 판매 중 this week 이번 주

[실시간 정답률] https://tinyurl.com/3cbck2p4
[해설] https://youtu.be/2w776wn5thg

5. Mr. Smith made a conservative guess at the population of the city.

[해석] 스미스 씨는 도시의 인구에 대해 보수적인 추정을 했다.

[어휘] make a guess 추정하다 conservative 보수적인 population 인구

[실시간 정답률] https://tinyurl.com/a3nr9h99
[해설] https://tinyurl.com/a3nr9h99

6. To meet our environmental goals, it is important that we reduce our carbon emissions.

[해석] 환경 목표를 달성하기 위해서는 우리의 탄소 배출을 줄이는 것이 중요하다.

[어휘] environmental goals 환경 목표 important 중요한 reduce 줄이다 carbon emissions 탄소 배출

[실시간 정답률] https://tinyurl.com/y7cbd94t
[해설] https://youtu.be/SqUUXsTh3UA

7. We have yet to receive the report although a promise has been made that it will arrive by the end of the day.

[해석] 그날의 끝까지 도착하기로 한 약속이 있었음에도 불구하고 보고서는 아직 도착하지 않았다.

[어휘] report 보고서 yet 아직 receive 받다 promise 약속 end of the day 그날의 끝

[실시간 정답률] https://tinyurl.com/5dw8j46v
[해설] https://youtu.be/yds0EXOHDH4

8. Zygo Corp made ------ updates to the Z-Car by incorporating a full-screen dashboard and facial recognition.

[해석] 지고 코퍼레이션은 전체 화면 대시보드와 안면 인식을 통합함으로써 Z-카에 상당한 업데이트를 했다.

[어휘] updates 업데이트 incorporate 통합하다 full-screen dashboard 전체 화면 대시보드 facial recognition 안면 인식 substantial 상당한

[실시간 정답률] https://tinyurl.com/3axsk2zm
[해설] https://youtu.be/gnhDNxv3EKY

9. We need an official permit at least one month ahead of the start of the construction project.

[해석] 건설 프로젝트 시작 최소한 한 달 전에 공식 허가가 필요하다.

[어휘] official permit 공식 허가 construction project 건설 프로젝트 ahead of ~전에

[실시간 정답률] https://tinyurl.com/37amu45d
[해설] https://youtu.be/ShBm45XhWUQ

10. Rather than offer high-end equipment, the Downtown Gym keeps its membership fees affordable to those who work out every day.

[해석] 고급 장비를 제공하는 것보다 다운타운 체육관은 매 운동하는 사람들에게 회원비를 저렴하게 유지한다.

[어휘] offer 제공하다 high-end 고급의 equipment 장비 keep 유지하다 membership 회원 fee 요금 affordable 저렴한

[실시간 정답률] https://tinyurl.com/5n6pvc7t
[해설] https://youtu.be/7n0Bo_c2eRA

해설

11. All employees are required to receive approval from their immediate supervisor before using company vehicles.

[해석] 모든 직원은 회사 차량을 사용하기 전에 직속 상관으로부터 승인을 받아야 한다.

[어휘] employee 직원 required 필요한 approval 승인 immediate supervisor 직속 상관 company vehicle 회사 차량

[실시간 정답률] https://tinyurl.com/83swfdks
[해설] https://youtu.be/oR-dfzKziko

12. The display cases in our stores makes our products attractive to customers.

[해석] 우리 매장의 진열대는 우리 제품을 소비자에게 매력적으로 보이게 한다.

[어휘] display case 진열대 store 매장 attractive 매력적인 customer 소비자

[실시간 정답률] https://tinyurl.com/398hn6ra
[해설] https://youtu.be/u5tYZUTswrM

13. The conference hall has a capacity of 500 people, making it ideal for large events and gatherings.

[해석] 컨퍼런스 홀은 500명의 수용력을 가지고 있어, 큰 행사와 모임에 이상적이다.

[어휘] conference hall 대 회의실 capacity 수용력 ideal 이상적인 gatherings 모임들

[실시간 정답률] https://tinyurl.com/a3nr9h99
[해설] https://youtu.be/k-vdczyjVnQ

14. Due to weakening economic indicators, many businesses are reconsidering their expansion plans.

[해석] 경제 지표의 약화로 많은 기업들이 확장 계획을 재고하고 있다.

[어휘] due to ~때문에 weakening 약화 economic indicator 경제 지표 many 많은 business 기업 reconsider 재고하다 expansion plan 확장 계획

[실시간 정답률] https://tinyurl.com/272e79zv
[해설] https://youtu.be/qmqBA6W0P-c

15. The Paradise Spa & Resort is now offering a 30-percent discount on repeat customers.

[해석] 파라다이스 스파 & 리조트는 이제 단골 고객에게 30퍼센트 할인을 제공하고 있다.

[어휘] offer 제공하다 discount 할인 repeat customer 단골 고객

[실시간 정답률] https://tinyurl.com/493t6rmj
[해설] https://youtu.be/NQNWu2tOXa0

16. The newly designed helmet will better protect workers from head injuries.

[해석] 새롭게 디자인 된 헬멧은 근로자들이 머리 부상으로부터 더 잘 보호받을 수 있도록 할 것이다.

[어휘] newly 새롭게 helmet 헬멧 better 더 잘 protect 보호하다 workers 근로자들 head injuries 머리 부상

[실시간 정답률] https://tinyurl.com/43w4cvhy
[해설] https://youtu.be/3XFsHfHfpDs

17. Mr. Frank praised the sales team for successfully securing a lucrative contract yesterday.

[해석] 프랭크 씨는 어제 수익성 높은 계약을 성공적으로 얻어낸 것에 대해 영업 팀을 칭찬했다.

[어휘] praise 칭찬하다 sales team 영업 팀 successfully 성공적으로 lucrative contract 수익성 높은 계약

[실시간 정답률] https://tinyurl.com/yc8r9tvt
[해설] https://youtu.be/ck_n3C3m_Qc

18. Maria headed to the pharmacy to pick up her prescribed medicine.

[해석] 마리아는 처방받은 약을 받으러 약국에 갔다.

[어휘] head to ~로 가다 pharmacy 약국 pick up 받다 prescribed 처방받은 medicine 약

[실시간 정답률] https://tinyurl.com/332yzhcv
[해설] https://youtu.be/BSXBPlaqtHk

19. Through these updates, users may no longer need to enter a password when prompted.

[해석] 이 업데이트를 통해 사용자들은 암호를 요청받을 때 입력할 필요가 없을지도 모른다.

[어휘] updates 업데이트 password 비밀번호 when prompted 요청받을 때

[실시간 정답률] https://tinyurl.com/4zevvw79
[해설] https://youtu.be/yuNyGmfqb0M

20. Mr. Norakai wasn't able to attend the seminar on May 1, since he was sick at the time.

[해석] 노라카이 씨는 당시 아팠기 때문에 5월 1에 열린 세미나에 참석할 수 없었다.

[어휘] attend 참석하다 seminar 세미나 since ~ 때문에 sick 아픈

[실시간 정답률] https://tinyurl.com/bdduu2cy
[해설] https://youtu.be/1RN9iv3YkIk

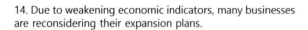

21. The blades of the fan should not be washed under running water. Instead, delicately dust them off with a soft brush.

[해석] 선풍기의 날개는 흐르는 물에 씻어서는 안 됩니다. 대신 부드러운 브러시로 조심스럽게 먼지를 털어내세요.

[어휘] blades 날개 running water 흐르는 물, 수돗물 instead 대신에 delicately 조심스럽게 dust off 먼지를 털어내다

[실시간 정답률] https://tinyurl.com/4zpmxtay
[해설] https://youtu.be/HVpWlO2moKo

22. Due to the ongoing repaving work in the underground parking area, we kindly request your patience and understanding.

[해석] 지하 주차장에서 진행 중인 포장 공사로 인해, 당신의 인내심과 이해를 부탁드립니다.

[어휘] ongoing 진행 중인 repaving work 포장 공사 underground 지하 parking area 주차장 kindly 친절히 request 요청하다 patience 인내심 understanding 이해

[실시간 정답률] https://tinyurl.com/5b7c6ebx
[해설] https://youtu.be/ktTJP-BruOc

23. Unless there's a factory inspection scheduled for today, all product shipments will be delayed by one day this week.

[해석] 오늘 공장 검사가 예정되어 있기 때문에, 이번 주 모든 제품 출하는 하루 지연될 것이다.

[어휘] unless ~하지 않는 한 factory 공장 inspection 검사 scheduled 예정된 product 제품 shipment 출하 delayed 지연되는 one day 하루

[실시간 정답률] https://tinyurl.com/yajnyhnd
[해설] https://youtu.be/f75-quni-Z8

24. Having received the same wage for two years, Mr. Son was happy that his hard work had been recognized with a pay raise.

[해석] 두 해 동안 같은 임금을 받았던 손 씨는 임금 인상으로 자신의 수고가 인정받아 기뻤다.

[어휘] same 같은 wage 임금 receive 받다 hard work 수고 be recognized 인정받다 pay raise 임금 인상

[실시간 정답률] https://tinyurl.com/n3dat6j3
[해설] https://youtu.be/HqDl492V6WA

25. Onsite childcare services among many perks at Apex Solutions are provided only for night shift workers.

[해석] Apex Solutions의 여러 혜택 중 현장 어린이 보육 서비스는 야간 근무자들만을 위해 제공된다.

[어휘] onsite 현장의 childcare 어린이 보육 perk 혜택 night shift 야간 근무

[실시간 정답률] https://tinyurl.com/y2c8tba3
[해설] https://youtu.be/_J5PVPrZKc0

26. The initiative encourages the community to monitor and report on climate change along the coastline.

[해석] 이 계획은 지역 사회가 해안선을 따라 기후 변화를 모니터링하고 보고하도록 장려한다.

[어휘] initiative 이니셔티브 engages 참여시키다 community 지역 사회 monitor 모니터링하다 report 보고하다 climate change 기후 변화 coastline 해안선

[실시간 정답률] https://tinyurl.com/532k5j2d
[해설] https://youtu.be/fYZS6_oUlUc

27. Attached, please find my professional portfolio for your consideration.

[해석] 첨부된 문서에서 제 전문 포트폴리오를 검토해 주시기 바랍니다.

[어휘] attached 첨부된 professional 포트폴리오 consideration 검토

[실시간 정답률] https://tinyurl.com/ya9jf8ze
[해설] https://youtu.be/02VHDco6dL8

28. Chef Rivera opted to lightly dress the salad with olive oil and lemon for a fresh, zesty flavor.

[해석] 셰프 리베라는 신선하고 풍미가 강한 맛을 위해 올리브 오과 레몬으로 샐러드를 가볍게 드레싱하기로 선택했다.

[어휘] opt to ~하기로 선택하다 lightly 가볍게 dress 드레싱하다 salad 샐러드 olive oil 올리브 오 lemon 레몬 fresh 신선한 zesty 풍미가 강한 flavor 맛

[실시간 정답률] https://tinyurl.com/2p94kwaj
[해설] https://youtu.be/s6DW8Tbazmw

29. Following the guidelines in MK Fashion magazine can make you look stunning in your professional outfits.

[해석] MK 패션 매거진의 지침을 따르면 당신의 전문적인 복장에서 놀라운 모습으로 보 수 있다.

[어휘] guideline 지침 make 만들다 look 보이다 stunning 놀라운 professional 전문적인 outfit 복장

[실시간 정답률] https://tinyurl.com/re6cnyfw
[해설] https://youtu.be/5F8y9ukg-A0

30. The morning meeting, at which they presented their quarterly results, was attended by top executives.

[해석] 그들이 분기별 결과를 발표했던 아침 회의는 최고 경영진이 참석했다.

[어휘] morning meeting 아침 회의 quarterly results 분기별 결과 attend 참석하다 top executives 최고 경영진

[실시간 정답률] https://tinyurl.com/mud22r8v
[해설] https://youtu.be/dl43Ys-R6fY

해설

31. Our program offers training sessions targeted at young entrepreneurs to develop their business skills.

[해석] 우리 프로그램은 젊은 창업가들이 사업 능력을 개발할 수 있도록 의도된 훈련 세션을 제공한다.

[어휘] program 프로그램 training sessions 훈련 세션 targeted 의도된, 목표로 하여진 entrepreneurs 창업가

[실시간 정답률] https://tinyurl.com/2v5m38bj
[해설] https://youtu.be/6rfuW1HwJxw

32. Hunting activities are subject to control by wildlife conservation agencies to ensure sustainable practices.

[해석] 사냥 활동은 지속 가능한 관행을 보장하기 위해 야생 보호 기관에 의해 규제 받는다.

[어휘] be subject to ~을 받다, ~에 의해 영향을 받다 control 규제, 통제 wildlife conservation agencies 야생 보호 기관 ensure 보장하다, 확실히 하다 sustainable practices 지속 가능한 관행

[실시간 정답률] https://tinyurl.com/5y65nujk
[해설] https://youtu.be/RFOjLnSocFY

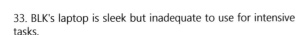

33. BLK's laptop is sleek but inadequate to use for intensive tasks.

[해석] BLK의 랩톱은 세련되었지만 강도 높은 작업에 사용하기에는 부적합하다.

[어휘] laptop 랩톱 sleek 세련된 inadequate 부적합한 intensive 강도 높은 tasks 작업

[실시간 정답률] https://tinyurl.com/3v3ppy2j
[해설] https://youtu.be/FNWNagQxCh0

34. To ensure safety, please read the operation protocols on our Web site before running the machinery.

[해석] 안전을 보장하기 위해 기계를 작동하기 전에 저희 웹사이트에 있는 운영 절차를 읽어 주십시오.

[어휘] ensure 보장하다 safety 안전 operation 운영 protocol 절차 running 작동 하는 것 machinery 기계

[실시간 정답률] https://tinyurl.com/phjsknre
[해설] https://youtu.be/ur5cDyHm8xU

35. The government decided to evacuate the houses around the mountain after the flood.

[해석] 홍수 후 정부는 산 주변의 집들을 대피시키기로 결정했다.

[어휘] evacuate 대피시키다 around 주변 flood 홍수

[실시간 정답률] https://tinyurl.com/mw9ukz6n
[해설] https://youtu.be/g4NXTEOPU_o

36. Along with technological advances also comes the opportunity to streamline manual work.

[해석] 기술적 진보와 함께 수동 작업을 간소화할 기회도 도래한다.

[어휘] along with ~와 함께 technological advances 기술적 진보 opportunity 기회 streamline 간소화하다 manual work 수동 작업

[실시간 정답률] https://tinyurl.com/verssbb9
[해설] https://youtu.be/qKdp3tYnNAU

37. A marketing expert was hired to help sales associates promote their ideas to prospect customers.

[해석] 마케팅 전문가가 고객에게 아이디어를 홍보할 수 있도록 영업 직원을 돕기 위해 고용되었다.

[어휘] promote 홍보하다 prospect 잠재적인

[실시간 정답률] https://tinyurl.com/yck9yyek
[해설] https://youtu.be/PgCEf6qkkCw

38. Some of the appliances in hotels are simple and functional as they are designed for durability rather than aesthetic purposes.

[해석] 호텔의 부 기기들은 미적 목적보다는 내구성을 위해 디자인되어 간단하고 기능적이다.

[어휘] appliance 기기 designed for ~을 위해 디자인되다 durability 내구성 aesthetic 미적인

[실시간 정답률] https://tinyurl.com/27aum6m3
[해설] https://youtu.be/vlZ0xUn_LJg

39. Moonlight Deliveries intends to move forward with the construction of a warehouse in Busan.

[해석] 문라이트 딜리버리는 부산에 창고를 건설하기 위해 계획을 진행할 예정이다.

[어휘] intend 의도하다 move forward with 진행하다 construction 건설 warehouse 창고

[실시간 정답률] https://tinyurl.com/35krzdcd
[해설] https://youtu.be/0VMSdskS1F0

40. Mr. Brown attributed his ability to make insightful investments to techniques he learned from his father.

[해석] 브라운 씨는 그의 통찰력 있는 투자 능력을 아버지에게서 배운 기술에 기인한다고 여겼다.

[어휘] attribute 기인하다 ability 능력 insightful 통찰력 있는 investment 투자 technique 기술 learn 배우다

[실시간 정답률] https://tinyurl.com/5n6ppfux
[해설] https://youtu.be/cP0lr5jdY0U

해설

41. Mr. Bake wrote an article urging the government to increase supervision of the nation's manufacturing sector.

[해석] 베이크 씨는 국가 제조 부문의 감독을 강화하도록 정부에 촉구하는 기사를 작성했다.

[어휘] write 작성하다 urge 촉구하다 increase 증가시키다 supervision 감독 manufacturing sector 제조 부문

[실시간 정답률] https://tinyurl.com/mr37arm2
[해설] https://youtu.be/4ZCx0UO7XKA

42. During the meeting, the manager spoke more softly than usual to maintain a calm atmosphere.

[해석] 회의 도중, 매니저는 평소보다 더 부드럽게 말하여 차분한 분위기를 유지했다.

[어휘] meeting 회의 speak 말하다 softly 부드럽게 usual 평소 maintain 유지하다 calm 차분한 atmosphere 분위기

[실시간 정답률] https://tinyurl.com/bdf7k84f
[해설] https://youtu.be/keKtwENngog

43. Thank you for joining our membership. Now, you will be the first to discover our exclusive content and offers. Expect to receive your detailed welcome message shortly.

[해석] 우리 멤버십에 가입해주셔서 감사합니다. 이제, 당신은 우리의 독점적인 콘텐츠와 제안을 가장 먼저 발견하게 될 것입니다. 곧 자세한 환영 메시지를 받게 될 것으로 기대하십시오.

[어휘] discover 발견하다 exclusive 독점적인 receive 받다

[실시간 정답률] https://tinyurl.com/2bvteub4
[해설] https://youtu.be/5ZjCfGff_Sk

44. Please be advised that critics do not always agree with the views of Northeast News and Post or the general public.

[해석] 평론가들은 북동 뉴스 포스트지나 대중의 견해에 항상 동의하는 것은 아닐 수 있음을 알아두세요.

[어휘] Please be advised 알아두세요 critic 평론가 not always 항상 ~인 것만은 아니다 view 견해 Northeast News and Post 북동 뉴스 포스트 general public 대중

[실시간 정답률] https://tinyurl.com/myjpkwa4
[해설] https://youtu.be/jOsAJszEPqo

45. In order to provide continuity, the board of directors asked Mr. Gu to extend his stay as CEO.

[해석] 연속성을 제공하기 위해, 이사회는 구 씨에게 CEO로서의 재임을 연장해달라고 요청했다.

[어휘] provide 제공하다 continuity 연속성 board of directors 이사회 extend 연장하다

[실시간 정답률] https://tinyurl.com/3dp4nmkt
[해설] https://youtu.be/8cRIe6O-rLk

46. Mr. Arroyo worked for more than a decade at the Easton Group before joining Sunflower Houseware Ltd.

[해석] 아로요 씨는 선플라워 하우스웨어 주식회사에 합류하기 전에 10년 이상 이스턴 그룹에서 했다.

[어휘] work 하다 decade 십년 before 전에 join 합류하다

[실시간 정답률] https://tinyurl.com/rp96rpt9
[해설] https://youtu.be/wPeqnwl-jVU

47. Formerly a renowned pianist, Ms. Park now runs a bookstore.

[해석] 예전에 유명한 피아니스트였던 박 씨는 지금 서점을 운영한다.

[어휘] formerly 예전에 renowned 유명한 pianist 피아니스트 run 운영하다 bookstore 서점

[실시간 정답률] https://tinyurl.com/29hxhk4a
[해설] https://youtu.be/zWsdjEu9MPY

48. Archaeologists excavate old tombs and study their historical meanings through various techniques.

[해석] 고고학자들은 오래된 무덤을 발굴하고 다양한 기술을 통해 그들의 역사적 의미를 연구한다.

[어휘] archaeologist 고고학자들 excavate 발굴하다 old 오래된 tombs 무덤 study 연구하다 historical 역사적인 meaning 의미 various 다양한 technique 기술

[실시간 정답률] https://tinyurl.com/3r733p3j
[해설] https://youtu.be/2xypHu5FOPo

49. Mr. Genistein had his car that stopped working during last night's heavy rain repaired.

[해석] 제네스타인 씨는 지난 밤의 폭우로 고장 난 자동차를 수리했다.

[어휘] stopped working 작동이 멈춘 during ~동안 last night's heavy rain 지난 밤의 폭우 repaired 수리된

[실시간 정답률] https://tinyurl.com/3z26z54b
[해설] https://youtu.be/TEQTZ4hI0Rk

50. The dinner invitations will be distributed right after they are checked for errors.

[해석] 저녁 초대장은 오류를 확인한 후 즉시 배포될 것입니다.

[어휘] dinner 저녁 invitation 초대장 distribute 배포하다 right after ~한 후 checked for errors 오류가 확인된

[실시간 정답률] https://tinyurl.com/5am3j7va
[해설] https://youtu.be/8eWVjshsGyw

해설

51. Artist Sebi MacDonad has been a creative force behind the city revitalization project since its inception.

[해석] 예술가 세비 맥도날드는 시작부터 도시 활성화 프로젝트의 창의적인 힘이 되어왔다.

[어휘] creative 창의적인 force 힘 revitalization 활성화 project 프로젝트 inception 시작

[실시간 정답률] https://tinyurl.com/2r6ffraa
[해설] https://youtu.be/dMCl5ld5l-c

52. Hearty Harvest supplies local stores in Seattle such as Harbor Grocers and Greenleaf Market.

[해석] Hearty Harvest는 Harbor Grocers와 Greenleaf Market과 같은 시애틀의 지역 상점에 식료품을 공급한다.

[어휘] supply 공급하다 cater to ~에 서비스를 제공하다 distribute 배포하다 contract with ~와 계약하다

[실시간 정답률] https://tinyurl.com/4fe2vstx
[해설] https://youtu.be/zVO0U1Ttiyw

53. The electronic version of our latest report is equivalent to the printed copy in terms of content and layout.

[해석] 최신 보고서의 전자 버전은 내용과 레이아웃 측면에서 인쇄본과 동등합니다.

[어휘] electronic version 전자 버전 latest 최신 report 보고서 equivalent 동등한 printed copy 인쇄본 in terms of ~측면에서 content 내용 layout 레이아웃

[실시간 정답률] https://tinyurl.com/2f45us87
[해설] https://youtu.be/q2KR6rK02SQ

54. Despite purchasing much fewer supplies, the Marketing Department spent most of its budget for the month.

[해석] 훨씬 적은 용품을 구매했음에도 불구하고, 마케팅 부서는 이번 달 예산의 대부분을 소비했다.

[어휘] despite ~에도 불구하고 purchasing 구매 much fewer 훨씬 적은 supplies 용품 spend 소비하다 most of its budget 이번 달 예산의 대부분

[실시간 정답률] https://tinyurl.com/4r6scm2x
[해설] https://youtu.be/MG5c_bKq1JA

55. The Oasis Video Book proved to be a very good alternative to Grape's N-pad Pro.

[해석] 오아시스 비디오 북은 그레이프의 N-패드 프로에 대한 매우 좋은 대안으로 판명되었다.

[어휘] prove to be ~라고 판명되다 alternative 대안

[실시간 정답률] https://tinyurl.com/y449asxv
[해설] https://youtu.be/maeJOOxcM3E

56. To keep productivity stable, the personnel manager should always attend to whichever department needs more employees.

[해석] 생산성을 안정적으로 유지하기 위해서, 인사 관리자는 직원이 더 필요한 부서에 항상 주의를 기울여야 한다.

[어휘] productivity 생산성 personnel manager 인사 관리자 attend to ~에 주의를 기울이다

[실시간 정답률] https://tinyurl.com/45mhwywr
[해설] https://youtu.be/lZC6eMWX-7c

57. Ms. Smith mentioned that the conference's complimentary breakfast was one appealing feature, while the free parking was another.

[해석] 스미스 씨는 회의의 무료 아침 식사가 매력적인 특징 중 하나라고 언급했으며, 무료 주차 또한 그러하다고 했다.

[어휘] complimentary 무료의 appealing 매력적인 feature 특징

[실시간 정답률] https://tinyurl.com/2vkdehxc
[해설] https://youtu.be/6nppfvKzVcA

58. Thomas Insurance's new policy provides full coverage against accidental damage to phones.

[해석] 토마스 보험의 새로운 정책은 전화기의 우발적 손상에 대해 전면적인 보상을 제공합니다.

[어휘] provide 제공하다 coverage 보상

[실시간 정답률] https://tinyurl.com/3yvfxhw6
[해설] https://youtu.be/Aw-LuSYs3AI

59. Company representatives receive compensation for attending the convention and are reimbursed for travel expenses.

[해석] 회사 대표들은 컨벤션에 참석하는 것에 대해 보상을 받으며 여행 경비는 환불 받는다.

[어휘] representative 대표 compensation 보상 attend 참석하다 convention 컨벤션 reimburse 환급해주다

[실시간 정답률] https://tinyurl.com/3w2r99xu
[해설] https://youtu.be/hHQphi7bR4E

60. Renowned for his expertise, Dr. Smith consistently keeps pace with the latest developments in his field.

[해석] 그의 전문 지식으로 유명한 스미스 박사는 그의 분야에서 최신 발전사항들 지속적으로 따라잡고 있다.

[어휘] renowned 유명한 expertise 전문 지식 keeps pace 따라잡다 developments 발전 사항들

[실시간 정답률] https://tinyurl.com/3bh634m9
[해설] https://youtu.be/lg8hrm2jk7s

해설

61. The Aqualab keeps its air conditions adequately moist for controlled experiments.

[해석] 아쿠아랩은 제어된 실험을 위해 그들의 공기 상태를 적절히 습기 있게 유지한다.

[어휘] keep 유지하다 air condition 공기 상태 adequately 적절히 moist 습기 있는 controlled experiment 제어된 실험

[실시간 정답률] https://tinyurl.com/59y94ftk
[해설] https://youtu.be/MSwUlty-H68

62. Yummy Foodland has pledged to respond to local charities' needs with annual profits.

[해석] Yummy Foodland는 연간 수익으로 지역 자선 단체의 요구에 응답하기로 약속했다.

[어휘] pledged 약속하다 respond 응답하다 local 지역의 charity 자선 단체 needs 요구 annual 연간의 profits 수익

[실시간 정답률] https://tinyurl.com/4rszn6d2
[해설] https://youtu.be/Fx31h-GDKYE

63. Until the main air-conditioning unit is fixed, workers are allowed to use their own cooling devices.

[해석] 주 에어컨 수리가 완료될 때까지 직원들은 자신의 냉각 장치를 사용할 수 있다.

[어휘] until ~할 때까지 main air conditioning unit 주 에어컨 cooling devices 냉각 장치

[실시간 정답률] https://tinyurl.com/2ffanbw6
[해설] https://youtu.be/-Rxs6ojSfcM

64. To show appreciation for your loyalty, we sent you a certificate for $200.

[해석] 귀하의 충성심에 대한 감사의 표시로, 우리는 귀하에게 200달러 상당의 상품권을 보냈습니다.

[어휘] appreciation 감사 loyalty 충성심 send 보내다 certificate 상품권

[실시간 정답률] https://tinyurl.com/2xwvu5r4
[해설] https://youtu.be/wQRlzxlxBmA

65. The launch of an online marketplace has made local sellers excited about the prospect of reaching a wider customer base.

[해석] 온라인 장터의 출시로 지역 판매자들은 보다 넓은 고객층에 접근할 수 있는 전망에 들떴다.

[어휘] launch 출시 excited 흥분한 prospect 전망 reaching 도달하는 wider 더 넓은 customer base 고객층

[실시간 정답률] https://tinyurl.com/2ju2mu9k
[해설] https://youtu.be/yT7HhXVB_wk

66. Believed to be the next big breakthrough in technology, Intech's new product has attracted significant media attention.

[해석] 기술에서 다음 큰 돌파구로 여겨지는 인텍의 새 제품은 상당한 언론의 관심을 끌었다.

[어휘] believed 여겨지는 breakthrough 돌파구 technology 기술 attract 끌다 media 언론 attention 관심

[실시간 정답률] https://tinyurl.com/xt2xdkp9
[해설] https://youtu.be/Vgu9gX0Wzb0

67. At times, employees attend company-wide networking events and socialize with one another.

[해석] 때때로, 직원들은 회사 전체의 네트워킹 이벤트에 참석하고 서로 사교한다.

[어휘] at times 때때로 attend 참석하다 networking event 친목 활동 socialize 사교하다

[실시간 정답률] https://tinyurl.com/33az38wv
[해설] https://youtu.be/Rzeb9NEZTGg

68. While the firm has hired many new workers every month for the past 2 years, there are no signs of it doing so this month.

[해석] 회사는 지난 2년 동안 매달 많은 새 직원을 고용했지만, 이번 달에는 그럴 조짐이 보이지 않는다.

[어휘] while ~하는 반면 firm 회사 hired 고용하다 workers 직원 signs 조짐

[실시간 정답률] https://tinyurl.com/pnhhvv96
[해설] https://youtu.be/YRRr45BFtKM

69. The library updated its collection, opting to include more digital resources over traditional books.

[해석] 도서관은 그들의 컬렉션을 업데이트하면서 전통적인 책보다는 디지털 자원을 더 포함하기로 선택했다.

[어휘] library 도서관 update 업데이트하다 collection 소장 도서 opt to ~를 선택하다 include 포함하다 digital resources 디지털 자원 traditional 전통적인

[실시간 정답률] https://tinyurl.com/bdz3hfzh
[해설] https://youtu.be/O_3nK0HsyJ8

70. All tours of the new art museum will be preceded by a short meeting with a guide.

[해석] 새 미술관의 모든 관람은 안내자와의 짧은 미팅이 선행될 것이다.

[어휘] tours 관람 be preceded by ~에 선행하다 guide 안내자

[실시간 정답률] https://tinyurl.com/r4tmx8xm
[해설] https://youtu.be/joOUtEU_QBA

해설

71. The HR department will conduct a seminar on office sustainability measures at 2:00 next Monday.

[해석] 인사부는 다음 주 월요 오후 2시에 사무실 지속 가능성 조치에 대한 세미나를 진행할 것이다.

[어휘] HR department 인사부 conduct 진행하다 seminar 세미나 sustainability 지속 가능성 measures 조치

[실시간 정답률] https://tinyurl.com/5ykyem2k
[해설] https://youtu.be/eKUlkaYUWj0

72. Ms. Taylor will chair the annual charity gala, over which the city council has granted her full organizational discretion.

[해석] 테러 씨는 시의회로부터 전체 조직에 대한 재량을 부여받은 연례 자선 갈라의 의장을 맡게 될 것이다.

[어휘] chair 의장을 맡다 annual 연례의 charity 자선 gala 갈라 city council 시의회 grant 부여하다 organizational 조직의 discretion 재량

[실시간 정답률] https://tinyurl.com/33xxjkze
[해설] https://youtu.be/wq5sUFzcDY0

73. Whenever we are unable to accommodate diners indoors, we seat them in our outdoor patio area.

[해석] 손님들을 실내에 앉힐 수 없을 때마다 야외 파티오 구역에 앉힌다.

[어휘] accommodate 수용하다 diners 식사하는 사람들 outdoor patio area 야외 파티오 구역

[실시간 정답률] https://tinyurl.com/bdfrdxsw
[해설] https://youtu.be/_WFj_bd5cYw

74. Mr. Johnson's professionalism and dedication to his work were widely praised by colleagues and industry leaders.

[해석] 존슨 씨의 전문성과 직무에 대한 헌신은 동료들과 산업 리더들에 의해 널리 칭찬받았다.

[어휘] professionalism 전문성 dedication 헌신 work 작업 widely praised 널리 칭찬받는 colleague 동료 industry leader 업계 리더

[실시간 정답률] https://tinyurl.com/4e7cuscr
[해설] https://youtu.be/XpGEQqz7YVY

75. Mr. Jeon decided to work as an intern as it had the potential to result in a full-time position.

[해석] 전 씨는 인턴으로 일하기로 결정했는데, 이는 정규직으로 이어질 가능성이 있었기 때문이다.

[어휘] potential 가능성 result in 결과가 되다 full-time position 정규직 자리

[실시간 정답률] https://tinyurl.com/242nwzua
[해설] https://youtu.be/watch?v=4OXQcmeu2Dw

76. Since early checkouts are considered cancelations, full cancelations fees can be charged.

[해석] 조기 체크아웃은 취소로 간주되므로 전액 취소 수수료가 부과될 수 있다.

[어휘] early checkout 조기 체크아웃 considere 간주하다 cancelation 취소 fee 수수료 charge 부과하다

[실시간 정답률] https://tinyurl.com/3un7xtba
[해설] https://youtu.be/watch?v=rnByjOe-7CE

77. The eagerly anticipated renovation of the city library was made possible thanks to a private donation.

[해석] 사적 기부 덕분에 기대를 모았던 시립 도서관의 개조가 가능해졌다.

[어휘] eagerly anticipated 간절히 기다려진 renovation 개조 possible 가능한 donation 기부

[실시간 정답률] https://tinyurl.com/3539txme
[해설] https://youtu.be/FMQPin0Xm5Q

78. It is imperative that the company procure essential supplies without further delay.

[해석] 회사는 추가 지연 없이 필수 물품을 확보해야 한다.

[어휘] company 회사 imperative 필수적인 procure 확보하다 essential 필수 supplies 물품 without further delay 추가 지연 없이

[실시간 정답률] https://tinyurl.com/nshpywmf
[해설] https://youtu.be/fxaG4bkZRxA

79. In Ms. Johnson's absence, the marketing coordinator is responsible for managing the campaign strategy.

[해석] 존슨 씨가 결석한 동안, 마케팅 코디네이터는 캠페인 전략을 관리하는 책임이 있다.

[어휘] absence 결석 marketing coordinator 마케팅 코디네이터 responsible 책임이 있는 campaign strategy 캠페인 전략

[실시간 정답률] https://tinyurl.com/2vdwkfkh
[해설] https://youtu.be/zoeiyZkvxc8

80. Tomorrow, our team will gather for the second time since the start of the new project.

[해석] 내, 우리 팀은 새 프로젝트 시작 이후 두 번째로 모 것이다.

[어휘] gather 모이다 second time 두 번째 since ~이후 start 시작 new project 새 프로젝트

[실시간 정답률] https://tinyurl.com/4uyt3pzd
[해설] https://youtu.be/9Q4DFzGKB4k

해설

81. We do not refund any damages caused by misuse, improper handling, or other user carelessness.

[해석] 우리는 오용, 부적절한 취급, 또는 다른 사용자의 부주의로 인한 손해에 대해 환불하지 않습니다.

[어휘] refund 환불하다 damage 손해 caused by ~에 의해 발생된 misuse 오용 improper 부적절한 handling 취급 other 다른 carelessness 부주의

[실시간 정답률] https://tinyurl.com/2s36cjut
[해설] https://youtu.be/8Y3uGSS8CxI

82. At times, the King Hotel could reach its full capacity, particularly when nationwide events take place.

[해석] 때때로, 킹 호텔은 전국적인 행사가 열릴 때 특히 한계 수용 능력에 도달할 수 있다.

[어휘] at times 때때로 full capacity 한계 수용 능력 particularly 특히 nationwide 전국적인

[실시간 정답률] https://tinyurl.com/4r8mxhat
[해설] https://youtu.be/Cywy4PeAh9M

83. The developers document changes for the upcoming software update.

[해석] 개발자들은 다가오는 소프트웨어 업데이트를에 적용되는 변경 사항을 문서화한다.

[어휘] developer 개발자 document 문서화하다 change 변경 사항 upcoming 다가오는

[실시간 정답률] https://tinyurl.com/4kekffva
[해설] https://youtu.be/5HTrmWFLaX8

84. When the date for the annual shareholders' meeting has been confirmed, the organizing committee will send out the invitations.

[해석] 연례 주주총회의 정이 확정되면, 조직위원회가 초대장을 발송할 것이다.

[어휘] annual 연례 shareholders' meeting 주주총회 confirm 확정하다 organizing committee 조직위원회 send out 발송하다 invitation] 초대장

[실시간 정답률] https://tinyurl.com/2stsc7fr
[해설] https://youtu.be/SNcOuV--MYo

85. We are looking for experienced, outgoing customer service representatives to handle inquiries during our peak business hours.

[해석] 우리는 바쁜 영업 시간 동안 문의를 처리할 경험 많고 외향적인 고객 서비스 직원을 찾고 있다.

[어휘] outgoing 외향적인 representative 직원 inquiries 문의 peak hours 가장 바쁜 시간

[실시간 정답률] https://tinyurl.com/mpxnyfup
[해설] https://youtu.be/xXPij_GKo_s

86. The International Association of Structures represents the interests of architects all around the world.

[해석] 국제 건축 협회는 전 세계 건축가들의 이익을 대변한다.

[어휘] represent 대변하다, 대표하다 interests 이익 architect 건축가

[실시간 정답률] https://tinyurl.com/3tt6pu3p
[해설] https://youtu.be/r62tJduWhUw

87. The lecture was delivered in an engaging manner, making the complex topic both understandable and interesting to the audience.

[해석] 강의는 참여를 유도하는 방식으로 진행되어 복잡한 주제를 청중에게 이해하기 쉽고 흥미롭게 만들었다.

[어휘] deliver 전달하다 engaging 참여를 유도하는 manner 방식 complex 복잡한

[실시간 정답률] https://tinyurl.com/3fsmw5s4
[해설] https://youtu.be/A9UgVu2f15w

88. All outgoing products at SIM Tech are tested under deliberately harsh conditions to ensure reliability.

[해석] SIM Tech의 모든 출고 제품은 신뢰성을 보장하기 위해 고의적으로 가혹한 조건 하에서 테스트된다.

[어휘] outgoing 출고된 product 제품 under ~하에서 deliberately 고의적으로 harsh 가혹한 conditions 조건 ensure 보장하다 reliability 신뢰성

[실시간 정답률] https://tinyurl.com/55x39bwn
[해설] https://youtu.be/CZFXhibP8Ww

89. The waitstaff at the restaurant greeted the guests with so much enthusiasm that they felt invigorated.

[해석] 식당의 웨이트스태프는 매우 열정적으로 손님을 맞아서 그들은 활력이 있게 느꼈다.

[어휘] waitstaff 웨이트스태프 greet 맞이하다 invigorated 활력있는

[실시간 정답률] https://tinyurl.com/mnmm9ndt
[해설] https://youtu.be/j7B22m-zOuw

90. More demand for sustainable packaging has prompted many companies to explore eco-friendly alternatives.

[해석] 지속 가능한 포장에 대한 더큰 수요는 많은 회사들이 친환경 대안을 탐색하도록 촉발시켰다.

[어휘] demand 수요 sustainable 지속 가능한 packaging 포장 prompt 유도하다 explore 탐색하다 eco-friendly 친환경적인 alternative 대안

[실시간 정답률] https://tinyurl.com/3fp5z8et
[해설] https://youtu.be/gnhDNxv3EKY

해설

91. HY Industries engineers gave a facility tour to ten new recruits that were hired on the same day.

[해석] HY 산업의 엔지니어들은 그 날 고용된 십 명의 신입직원들에게 시설 견학을 제공했다.

[어휘] engineer 엔지니어 facility tour 시설 견학 new recruits 신입직원들

[실시간 정답률] https://tinyurl.com/bp822yhk
[해설] https://youtu.be/U2xgengcYy8

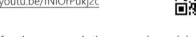

92. It is not clear how persuasive Adam Smith can be when he delivers a talk in front of a large audience.

[해석] 아담 스미스가 큰 청중 앞에서 연설을 할 때 그가 얼마나 설득력이 있을지 명확하지 않다.

[어휘] persuasive 설득력 있는 delivers 연설하다 audience 청중

[실시간 정답률] https://tinyurl.com/37abjaua
[해설] https://youtu.be/fNlOrPukj2c

93. The idea for the new marketing campaign originated from a brainstorming session during the meeting.

[해석] 새 마케팅 캠페인의 아이디어는 회의 중 브레인스토밍 세션에서 비롯되었다.

[어휘] campaign 캠페인 originate 비롯되다 brainstorming 브레인스토밍 session 시간의 한 구획 meeting 회의

[실시간 정답률] https://tinyurl.com/44446vju
[해설] https://youtu.be/rbWn0ZVDBpQ

94. Please have these copies of the handout sent to the sales manager.

[해석] 영업 관리자에게 이 자료집을 보내주시기 바랍니다.

[어휘] several 여러 copies 복사 handout 자료집

[실시간 정답률] https://tinyurl.com/3zvw39wb
[해설] https://youtu.be/qLr1AnW0BHA

95. Ms. Hedy's absence comes as something of a surprise, considering she has never been late for any meeting.

[해석] 헤디 씨의 결석은 그녀가 어떤 회의에도 지각한 적이 없다는 것을 고려하면 놀라운 이다.

[어휘] absence 결석 surprise 놀람 considering 고려하면 late 늦은 meeting 회의

[실시간 정답률] https://tinyurl.com/2r9f6z5r
[해설] https://youtu.be/vHJSyJsgi4w

96. Employees who work remotely fear being forgotten and nevertheless receive the same opportunities as those who don't.

[해석] 원격으로 하는 직원들은 잊혀질까 두려워하지만 그럼에도 불구하고 출근하는 직원들과 동한 기회를 받는다.

[어휘] remotely 원격으로 fear 두려워하다 forgotten 잊혀진 nevertheless 그럼에도 불구하고 opportunity 기회

[실시간 정답률] https://tinyurl.com/vwjatsfp
[해설] https://youtu.be/XmocxVQuu_k

97. Nordisk Industry's employees can be reimbursed for their tuition if they want to complete a program in higher education.

[해석] 노르디스크 산업의 직원들은 고등 교육 프로그램을 완료하고자 한다면 수업료를 환급받을 수 있다.

[어휘] reimburse 환급하다 tuition 수업료 complete 완료하다
[실시간 정답률] https://tinyurl.com/2dvvnt6m
[해설] https://youtu.be/FXQMUwUFnnY

98. Kangaroos are indigenous to many regions of Australia but are infrequently observed in residential neighborhoods.

[해석] 캥거루는 호주의 많은 지역에 서식하지만 주거 지역에서는 드물게 관찰된다.

[어휘] indigenous 토착의 infrequently 드물게

[실시간 정답률] https://tinyurl.com/yc2ex5mj
[해설] https://youtu.be/vKzjopCrgLs

99. Ms. Patel's rapport with her clients significantly increased her account retention rates.

[해석] 파텔 씨의 고객과의 좋은 관계는 그녀의 고객 계정 유지율을 크게 증가시켰다.

[어휘] rapport 긴밀한 관계 retention 유지

[실시간 정답률] https://tinyurl.com/5djf9cdh
[해설] https://youtu.be/aRte1UAMwps

100. We will talk about how we can increase a livestream's viewership.

[해석] 우리는 라이브스트림의 시청자 수를 어떻게 늘릴 수 있을지에 대해 논의할 것이다.

[어휘] livestream 라이브스트림 increase 늘리다 viewership 시청자 수

[실시간 정답률] https://tinyurl.com/ycy6mm4a
[해설] https://youtu.be/xTOW3Ip_fMA

해설

101. Fujiwara Automotive is committed to employee retention and advancement to management positions.

[해석] 후지와라 자동차는 직원 유지와 관리직 자리로의 승진에 진심이다.

[어휘] be committed to ~에 전념하다 employee 직원 retention 유지 advancement 승진 management 경영(진) position 자리, 위치

[실시간 정답률] https://tinyurl.com/3ypkrhpd
[해설] https://youtu.be/RJqlTcRegQo

102. Those remaining in the building received instructions to proceed to the nearest exit.

[해석] 건물에 남아있는 사람들은 가장 가까운 출구로 나가가라는 지시를 받았다.

[어휘] remaining 남아있는 instruction 지시 proceed 나아가다 nearest 가장 가까운 exit 출구
[실시간 정답률] https://tinyurl.com/452d7sdu
[해설] https://youtu.be/8lKyZz7KWhw

103. Light meals are typically delivered free of charge to office workers within the city limits.

[해석] 가벼운 식사는 도시 이내에서 사무실 근로자들에게 반적으로 무료로 배달된다.

[어휘] light meals 가벼운 식사 typically 반적으로, 전형적으로 deliver 배달하다 free of charge 무료로 office workers 사무실 근로자들 city limits 도시 한계

[실시간 정답률] https://tinyurl.com/msny6rer
[해설] https://youtu.be/c7c2uX5LwW4

104. The organization's objectives and missions are summarized succinctly in its vision statement.

[해석] 조직의 목표와 사명은 그 비전 성명서에 간결하게 요약되어 있다.

[어휘] objective 목표 mission 사명 summarize 요약하다 succinctly 간결하게

[실시간 정답률] https://tinyurl.com/wuvpaaxh
[해설] https://youtu.be/wghAGGTtMyw

105. Every two weeks, city work crews will collect green bins for such recyclables as glass bottles and aluminum cans.

[해석] 2주에 한번, 도시 작업반은 유리병과 알루미늄 캔 같은 재활용 가능한 물건들을 위해 녹색 쓰레기통을 수거할 것이다.

[어휘] collect 수거하다 green bins 녹색 쓰레기통 recyclables 재활용 가능한 물건들 glass bottle 유리병 aluminum can 알루미늄 캔

[실시간 정답률] https://tinyurl.com/23335uks
[해설] https://youtu.be/NHI__igvlnU

106. Almost all international school students are bilingual, and some of them can even speak three or more languages.

[해석] 대부분의 국제학교 학생들은 이중언어 사용자이며, 그 중 부는 세 개 이상의 언어를 할 수도 있다.

[어휘] international school students 국제학교 학생들 bilingual 이중언어 사용자 language 언어

[실시간 정답률] https://tinyurl.com/3kv9w6rc
[해설] https://youtu.be/qRnAMvnEvbY

107. If you don't have enough time to review the entire contract, please refer to a version without supporting documents.

[해석] 전체 계약을 검토할 충분한 시간이 없다면, 부속 문서 없는 버전을 참조해 주십시오.

[어휘] enough 충분한 review 검토 entire 전체 contract 계약 refer to 참고하다 version 버전 without ~없는 supporting documents 부속 문서, 증빙 문건

[실시간 정답률] https://tinyurl.com/mtucmu99
[해설] https://youtu.be/fu5SrFpoSnw

108. We are interested in knowing what the building's additions were to its facilities, including a new lounge.

[해석] 건물의 시설에 새로운 라운지를 포함하여, 무엇이 추가되었는지 알고 싶습니다.

[어휘] interested 관심 있는 building's 건물의 additions 추가물 facilities 시설 including 포함하여 lounge 라운지

[실시간 정답률] https://tinyurl.com/fjkmbe6d
[해설] https://youtu.be/n9SiCXv1k_M

109. Productivity in our office will stay consistent even if many employees work remotely next week.

[해석] 사무실 내 생산성은 심지어 다음 주에 많은 직원들이 원격으로 한다고 해도 관되게 유지될 것입니다.

[어휘] productivity 생산성 office 사무실 stay consistent 관되게 유지되다 even if 심지어 ~해도 remotely 원격으로

[실시간 정답률] https://tinyurl.com/3297wewx
[해설] https://youtu.be/MDNS_XmVRCY

110. Green energy usage is expanding across the globe even though many people still rely on fossil fuels.

[해석] 전 세계적으로 많은 사람들이 여전히 화석 연료에 의존하고 있음에도 불구하고 녹색 에너지 사용이 확대되고 있다.

[어휘] green energy 녹색 에너지 usage 사용 across the globe 전 세계에 걸쳐 rely on ~에 의존하다 fossil fuel 화석 연료

[실시간 정답률] https://tinyurl.com/9ej5p3r7
[해설] https://youtu.be/jaOa4yUjsCk

해설

111. According to the earnings projections, unless things change, the Crown Company will fall behind its competitors.

[해석] 수익 예측에 따르면, 상황이 바뀌지 않는 한 크라운 컴퍼니는 경쟁자들보다 뒤처질 것이다.

[어휘] earnings 수익 projections 예측 unless ~하지 않는 한 competitors 경쟁자들 fall behind 뒤처지다

[실시간 정답률] https://tinyurl.com/25cxu5yk
[해설] https://youtu.be/TuMCJnN_fTU

112. Kenshiro Motors's new compact model is well received because it has a spacious trunk without sacrificing interior space.

[해석] 켄시로 모터스의 새로운 소형 모델은 넓은 트렁크를 갖추고 있으면서도 내부 공간을 희생하지 않아 호평을 받고 있다.

[어휘] well received 호평 받는 spacious 넓은 sacrifice 희생하다 interior 내부 space 공간

[실시간 정답률] https://tinyurl.com/ysue5pc5
[해설] https://youtu.be/OcEReW6-5J0

113. Each salesperson on the team should provide the results of his or her monthly sales.

[해석] 팀의 각 영업 사원은 그들의 월별 판매 결과를 제공해야 한다.

[어휘] provide 제공하다 result 결과

[실시간 정답률] https://tinyurl.com/4jn9t972
[해설] https://youtu.be/qvOzYVCDnZE

114. The passengers waiting to board the train bound for Busan were informed that theirs would arrive 15 minutes late.

[해석] 부산행 열차에 탑승하기 위해 기다리는 승객들은 기차가 15분 늦게 도착할 것이라는 통보를 받았다.

[어휘] passengers 승객 waiting 기다리는 board 탑승하다 train 기차 bound for ~행 inform 통보하다, 알리다 would ~할 것이다 arrive 도착하다 minutes 분 late 늦게

[실시간 정답률] https://tinyurl.com/mryykrd
[해설] https://youtu.be/eCjcOMsmPec

115. When the printer is jammed or otherwise malfunctions, an error message will be displayed on the control panel.

[해석] 프린터가 막히거나 그와는 다르게 오작동할 경우, 제어판에 오류 메시지가 표시됩니다.

[어휘] printer 프린터 be jammed 막히다 otherwise 그와는 달리 malfunctions 오작동하다 error 오류 display 표시하다 control panel 제어판

[실시간 정답률] https://tinyurl.com/56kzmfuk
[해설] https://youtu.be/hSknG4_mCJo

116. Mr. Goodwill should take another look at the manuscript before submitting it to the publisher.

[해석] 굿윌 씨는 출판사에 원고를 제출하기 전에 다시 한번 확인해야 한다.

[어휘] manuscript 원고 submit 제출하다 publisher 출판사

[실시간 정답률] https://tinyurl.com/mr2fw5ex
[해설] https://youtu.be/uP8tpzYl4Vk

117. Health Vision will determine, based on the outcomes of the upcoming clinical trials, if the new drug can be moved to the next phase of development.

[해석] 건강 비전은 다가오는 임상 시험의 결과를 기반으로 새로운 약이 다음 개발 단계로 이동할 수 있는지를 결정할 것이다.

[어휘] clinical trials 임상 시험 outcome 결과 move 이동하다 phase 단계 development 개발
[실시간 정답률] https://tinyurl.com/mr2yz8a4
[해설] https://youtu.be/ST44j0yhgRM

118. Mr. Smith will oversee process innovation at the new facility in Chicago once the necessary team is assembled.

[해석] 필요한 팀이 구성되면 스미스 씨는 시카고의 새 시설에서 과정 혁신을 감독할 것이다.

[어휘] oversee 감독하다 process 과정 innovation 혁신 facility 시설 is assembled 구성되다

[실시간 정답률] https://tinyurl.com/t6htmcfx
[해설] https://youtu.be/roX_N31G4s0

119. As the business community has a great talent pool, anyone the HR manager picks will perform well.

[해석] 비즈니스 커뮤니티에는 훌륭한 인재 풀이 있어서 인사 관리자가 선택하는 누구든 잘 수행할 것이다.

[어휘] talent pool 인재 풀, 인재 집단 perform 수행하다

[실시간 정답률] https://tinyurl.com/bdhktt3n
[해설] https://youtu.be/yeGxDISspps

120. As the administration efficiently handled the implementation of the new policy, there was a notable increase in overall productivity.

[해석] 행정부가 새 정책의 시행을 효율적으로 처리하면서 전반적인 생산성이 눈에 띄게 증가했다.

[어휘] administration 행정부 efficiently 효율적으로 handle 처리하다 implementation 시행 productivity 생산성

[실시간 정답률] https://tinyurl.com/3sru6226
[해설] https://youtu.be/cxUP6kGXV48

해설

121. Because of a pipe leak in the lobby, the hotel shut down the area for the entire day.

[해석] 로비에서의 파이프 누수로 인해 호텔은 하루 종 그 지역을 폐쇄했습니다.

[어휘] because of ~때문에 leak 누수 shut down 폐쇄하다 the entire day 하루 전체의 날

[실시간 정답률] https://tinyurl.com/3fjm9w2b
[해설] https://youtu.be/9zoWVoPt-ok

122. When addressing customer complaints, service representatives must offer solutions, within reason, to ensure satisfaction and maintain loyalty.

[해석] 고객 불만을 해결할 때, 서비스 직원들은 합리적인 범위 내에서 만족과 충성 유지를 위해 해결책을 제공해야 합니다.

[어휘] address 처리하다 customer complaint 고객 불만 service representative 서비스 직원 offer 제공하다 solution 해결책 within reason 합리적인 범위 내에서 satisfaction 만족 maintain 유지하다 loyalty 충성

[실시간 정답률] https://tinyurl.com/v8s3tw8c
[해설] https://youtu.be/1bhZ_TQenx8

123. Orion Technologies' revenue was sufficient to cover most expenses this quarter.

[해석] 오리온 테크놀로지의 수익은 이번 분기 대부분의 비용을 충당하기에 충분했다.

[어휘] revenue 수익 sufficient 충분한 cover 충당하다 expense 비용

[실시간 정답률] https://tinyurl.com/5n82kn54
[해설] https://youtu.be/EYfAg5RaQi4

124. Please note that organic greens must be cleaned meticulously to ensure all residues are removed before they are eaten.

[해석] 유기농 채소는 먹기 전에 모든 잔류물이 제거되도록 세심하게 씻겨져야 함을 명심하세요.

[어휘] note 알다두다 organic 유기농 greens 채소 clean 청소하다 meticulously 세심하게 ensure 보장하다 residues 잔류물

[실시간 정답률] https://tinyurl.com/2hb6tjb8
[해설] https://youtu.be/meYF0DRzVZ0

125. While the one-day lecture Mr. Yang leads is very informative, it's the only one that provides role-playing activities and free consultations.

[해석] 양 씨가 이끄는 1 강의는 매우 유익한데 한편 역할극 활동과 무료 상담을 제공하는 유한 강의다.

[어휘] while ~하는 한편 one-day lecture 1 강의 informative 유익한 provide 제공하다 role-playing activities 역할극 활동 free consultation 무료 상담

[실시간 정답률] https://tinyurl.com/4fe355cp
[해설] https://youtu.be/8GPDal0TOKl

126. Fees in the local currency are subject to change due to fluctuating exchange rates.

[해석] 현지 화폐로 된 수수료는 변동하는 환율 때문에 변경될 수 있다.

[어휘] fee 수수료 local 현지 currency 화폐 subject to ~의 대상이다 change 변경 due to ~때문에 fluctuating 변동하는 exchange rates 환율

[실시간 정답률] https://tinyurl.com/4t2mrew9
[해설] https://youtu.be/-0H55tgBpkQ

127. Alphacore Solutions, as a last resort, closed the branch after exhausting all other options.

[해석] Alphacore Solutions는 다른 모든 옵션을 소진한 후 마지막 수단으로 지점을 폐쇄했습니다.

[어휘] resort 수단 exhaust 소진하다

[실시간 정답률] https://tinyurl.com/bp86xsrr
[해설] https://youtu.be/dJNzb_mZpb4

128. All employees are encouraged to contribute any good ideas to make their work environmentally safe and friendly.

[해석] 모든 직원들은 작업 환경을 친환경적이고 안전하게 만들기 위한 좋은 아이디어를 제출하도록 격려된다.

[어휘] employees 직원들 encourage 격려하다 contribute 제출하다 environmentally 친환경적으로 safe 안전한 friendly 친근한

[실시간 정답률] https://tinyurl.com/3pjx54r6
[해설] https://youtu.be/xcNqCy1nq3U

129. The Do More Unlimited plan comes with free international calls to over 80 countries.

[해석] Do More Unlimited 요금제에는 80개국 이상으로의 무료 국제 전화가 포함되어 있다.

[어휘] The Do More Unlimited plan Do More Unlimited 요금제 free international calls 무료 국제 전화 over 80 countries 80개국 이상

[실시간 정답률] https://tinyurl.com/ytyxk9m4
[해설] https://youtu.be/X9RzCaxyneM

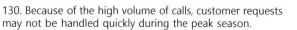

130. Because of the high volume of calls, customer requests may not be handled quickly during the peak season.

[해석] 전화 통화량이 많기 때문에 성수기 동안 고객의 요청이 신속하게 처리되지 않을 수 있다.

[어휘] volume 통화량 customer requests 고객 요청 peak season 성수기

[실시간 정답률] https://tinyurl.com/2yn6mfaj
[해설] https://youtu.be/zLPMTszLa7s

해설

131. Although the filmmaker almost rejected Sam Anderson, his movie ended up winning an award.

[해석] 비록 영화 제작자가 샘 앤더슨을 거의 거절할 뻔했지만 그의 영화는 결국 상을 받았다.

[어휘] filmmaker 영화 제작자 almost 거의 reject 거절하다 ended up 결국 ~로 끝나다 award 상 win 받다

[실시간 정답률] https://tinyurl.com/4jkeh8hh
[해설] https://youtu.be/71PBX0UAwel

132. Please advise that the copier on the third floor is temporarily out of service.

[해석] 3층의 복사기가 시적으로 고장 나있음을 알아두세요.

[어휘] advise 알리다 temporarily 임시로 out of service 고장 난

[실시간 정답률] https://tinyurl.com/5bmj8zks
[해설] https://youtu.be/IfqX1eCc4_w

133. A book signing is one of the many events that are happening in the course of the weeklong conference in Seoul.

[해석] 싸인회는 서울에서 열리는 주간의 컨퍼런스 과정 중 하나의 많은 행사입니다.

[어휘] book signing 싸인회 happening 어나고 있는 course 과정 weeklong 주간의 conference 컨퍼런스

[실시간 정답률] https://tinyurl.com/523fnutn
[해설] https://youtu.be/NoeJkbTLKEl

134. The restaurant owner was delighted that the new menu caused attract more customers.

[해석] 레스토랑 주인은 새로운 메뉴가 더 많은 고객을 유치하는 데 성공하여 기뻤습니다.

[어휘] restaurant owner 레스토랑 주인 delight 기쁘게 하다 new menu 새로운 메뉴 cause 유발하다 attract 끌어들이다

[실시간 정답률] https://tinyurl.com/yhuuppws
[해설] https://youtu.be/4Jiz8u2YakM

135. At the ceremony, Mr. Owen accepted a plaque in recognition of his contributions to the community.

[해석] 행사에서 오언 씨는 커뮤니티에 대한 그의 공헌을 인정받아 상패를 수여받았다.

[어휘] ceremony 행사 accept 수여받다 plaque 상패 recognition 인정 contribution 공헌

[실시간 정답률] https://tinyurl.com/2uuwe22e
[해설] https://youtu.be/FsVEd9nJxBg

136. Dr. Jones succinctly introduced the guests who were scheduled to present at the conference.

[해석] 존스 박사는 회의에서 발표할 예정인 게스트들을 간결하게 소개했다.

[어휘] succinctly 간결하게 introduce 소개하다 guest 초대 연설자 scheduled 예정된 present 발표하다 conference 회의

[실시간 정답률] https://tinyurl.com/mrx4y4eu
[해설] https://youtu.be/X7dyayKfWw8

137. Impressive as a good speaker, Mr. Smith never fails to captivate with eloquence and charisma.

[해석] 뛰어난 연설가로서, 스미스 씨는 말재주와 매력으로 사람을 매료시키는 데 실패한 적이 없다.

[어휘] good speaker 뛰어난 연설가 captivate 매료시키다 eloquence 말재주 charisma 매력 impressive 인상적인

[실시간 정답률] https://tinyurl.com/yp562shk
[해설] https://youtu.be/0elezAhsPUQ

138. To better serve our patients, our hospital offers a free reminder app with an easy-to-use calendar.

[해석] 환자들에게 더 나은 서비스를 제공하기 위해, 우리 병원은 사용하기 쉬운 달력이 있는 무료 알림 앱을 제공합니다.

[어휘] better serve 더 잘 모시다, 서비스하다 patient 환자 hospital 병원 offer 제공하다 free 무료 reminder 알림 app 애플리케이션 easy-to-use 사용하기 쉬운 calendar 달력

[실시간 정답률] https://tinyurl.com/2ad673uf
[해설] https://youtu.be/r_xe7_o3LAs

139. The FAQ page on our Web site has answers to the questions we get asked the most.

[해석] 우리 웹사이트의 FAQ 페이지에는 가장 자주 받는 질문에 대한 답변이 있습니다.

[어휘] FAQ 자주 묻는 질문 answer 답변 question 질문 most 가장

[실시간 정답률] https://tinyurl.com/3rnv7p47
[해설] https://youtu.be/wMb4tib_bTo

140. Mr. Kim will send the agenda for Friday's regular meeting before 5 o'clock today.

[해석] 김 씨는 오늘 5시 전에 금요 정기 회의의 안건을 보낼 것입니다.

[어휘] send 보내다 agenda 안건 regular meeting 정기 회의

[실시간 정답률] https://tinyurl.com/3utc5u7s
[해설] https://youtu.be/XMTZVNAOggg

해설

141. The lights went out just as the security guard was checking the area.

[해석] 보안 요원이 그 지역을 점검하고 있을 때 갑자기 불이 꺼졌다.

[어휘] light 불 go out 꺼지다 just as 딱 ~할 때 security guard 보안 요원 check 점검하다 area 지역

[실시간 정답률] https://tinyurl.com/7cd5wc7a
[해설] https://youtu.be/pKchHqS0J6s

142. Delightful Dining specializes in gourmet catering, not mass-produced, low-quality food options.

[해석] 딜라이트풀 다이닝은 대량 생산되지 않은 고급 케이터링에 전문화되어 있다.

[어휘] specialize in ~를 전문으로 하다 gourmet 고급의 catering 케이터링 mass-produced 대량 생산된 low-quality 저품질 food options 음식 선택

[실시간 정답률] https://tinyurl.com/y434yek4
[해설] https://youtu.be/6jq1Qp7dcUU

143. Daisy's Diner, most of whose dishes are enjoyed at its physical store, can be ordered online.

[해석] 데이지 다이너의 대부분의 요리는 매장에서 즐기지만 온라인으로 주문할 수 있다.

[어휘] dishes 요리 physical 물리적인 ordered 주문되다

[실시간 정답률] https://tinyurl.com/4p37dfbc
[해설] https://youtu.be/pjYdLxEUIrA

144. Last year, the committee created an award as there was a need to honor community-helping businesses.

[해석] 지난해, 위원회는 지역 사회를 돕는 기업을 기리기 위해 상을 만들었다.

[어휘] last year 지난해 committee 위원회 create 만들다 award 상 need 필요 honor 기리다 community helping 지역 사회를 돕는 businesses 기업

[실시간 정답률] https://tinyurl.com/mrphtcbj
[해설] https://youtu.be/4FQj_ieUACw

145. The widening of the road to a six-lane thoroughfare will ease the current traffic congestion in the area.

[해석] 도로를 6차선 도로로 확장하는 것은 해당 지역의 현재 교통 혼잡을 완화할 것이다.

[어휘] widening 확장 thoroughfare 도로 congestion 혼잡

[실시간 정답률] https://tinyurl.com/yfhcv256
[해설] https://youtu.be/mT3y6YIU2vk

146. Mr. Transkei filed a complaint form to the tech support team over a week ago.

[해석] 트랜스케이 씨는 주 이상 전에 기술 지원 팀에 불만 양식을 제출했다.

[어휘] file 제출하다 complaint form 불만 양식 tech support 기술 지원

[실시간 정답률] https://tinyurl.com/44ct5jrk
[해설] https://youtu.be/54g-nyRPXVg

147. Our president regards punctuality as a critical trait for successful sales associates to possess.

[해석] 우리 사장은 성공적인 영업 직원이 가져야 할 중요한 특성으로 시간엄수를 간주한다.

[어휘] regard 간주하다 punctuality 시간엄수 critical 중요한 trait 특성 successful 성공적인 sales associate 영업 직원

[실시간 정답률] https://tinyurl.com/mryy7kfw
[해설] https://youtu.be/0R2M1AkU6fs

148. The first salesperson to secure more than 100 contracts and receive the highest customer ratings will be honored at the awards ceremony.

[해석] 이번 시상식에서는 최초로 100개 이상의 계약을 확보하고 고객 평점을 가장 높게 받은 영업사원이 수상의 영예를 안게 된다.

[어휘] secure 확보하다 contracts 계약들 ratings 평가 honor 치하하다 awards ceremony 시상식

[실시간 정답률] https://tinyurl.com/y7ydp24d
[해설] https://youtu.be/nu6YtjedL88

149. The clean energy initiative was a success, proof that the team's dedication and expertise were instrumental.

[해석] 청정 에너지 이니셔티브는 성공적이었는데, 이는 팀의 헌신과 전문성이 중요한 역할을 했다는 증명이다.

[어휘] initiative 이니셔티브 prove 증명하다 instrumental 중요한

[실시간 정답률] https://tinyurl.com/8vbf3xap
[해설] https://youtu.be/watch?v=-IqYaTAAfAU

150. While most sales associates work in offices, some have the option to work remotely.

[해석] 대부분의 판매 직원들이 사무실에서 하는 반면, 부는 원격으로 하는 선택권을 가지고 있다.

[어휘] sales associate 판매 직원 work in offices 사무실에서 하다 some 부 option 선택권 work remotely 원격으로 하다

[실시간 정답률] https://tinyurl.com/8htc4jbt
[해설] https://youtu.be/pg8lHAhCONo

해설

151. The music event is offered free of charge, with beverages available for purchase from vending machines.

[해석] 음악 행사는 무료로 제공되며, 자판기에서 구매할 수 있는 음료가 있다.

[어휘] free of charge 무료로 beverage 음료 purchase 구매 vending machine 자판기

[실시간 정답률] https://tinyurl.com/2s56hrht
[해설] https://youtu.be/DZuBcppkrR0

152. Due to enhanced efficiency measures, there will be reductions by all departments in energy consumption.

[해석] 향상된 효율 조치로 인해, 모든 부서에서 에너지 소비가 감소될 것입니다.

[어휘] enhanced 향상된 efficiency 효율 measures 조치들 reduction 감소 energy consumption 에너지 소비

[실시간 정답률] https://tinyurl.com/bdf54uuh
[해설] https://youtu.be/BeMe_bJlqlc

153. If you need to buy a software package, select whichever integrates seamlessly with the existing system.

[해석] 소프트웨어 패키지를 구매해야 한다면, 기존 시스템과 완벽하게 통합되는 것을 선택하십시오.

[어휘] software package 소프트웨어 패키지 select 선택하다 integrate 통합하다 seamlessly 완벽하게 existing 기존의

[실시간 정답률] https://tinyurl.com/3j4nknff
[해설] https://youtu.be/WvS86fBnVG4

154. At the conference, Ms. Williams announced which strategies Orion Dynamics will implement to improve customer engagement.

[해석] 회의에서 윌리엄스 씨는 오리온 다이내믹스가 고객 참여를 개선하기 위해 실행할 전략들을 발표했다.

[어휘] strategy 전략 implement 실행하다 improve 개선하다 customer 고객 engagement 참여

[실시간 정답률] https://tinyurl.com/yynn8yt9
[해설] https://youtu.be/hZhx3rXVHgM

155. The board has approved a new policy dedicated to streamlining operational processes and reducing costs.

[해석] 이사회는 운영 과정을 간소화하고 비용을 절감하기 위한 새로운 정책을 승인했다.

[어휘] streamline 간소화하다 operational 운영의 reduce 줄이다 cost 비용

[실시간 정답률] https://tinyurl.com/mr2eyevz
[해설] https://youtu.be/LyH3g65r3WY

156. Ms. Shaniya recovered from her injuries just a few days before her 26th birthday.

[해석] 샤니야는 그녀의 26번째 생일 몇 일 전에 부상에서 회복되었다.

[어휘] recover 회복하다 injury 부상

[실시간 정답률] https://tinyurl.com/bdeeamsb
[해설] https://youtu.be/9oK6AHMc3f4

157. Using visual aids can help the audience fully grasp the presentation's main points.

[해석] 시각 자료를 사용하면 청중이 발표의 주요 포인트를 완전히 이해하는 데 도움이 될 수 있다.

[어휘] using 사용하다 visual aids 시각 자료 help 도움이 되다 audience 청중 fully 완전히 grasp 이해하다 presentation 발표 main points 주요 포인트

[실시간 정답률] https://tinyurl.com/22jn8m3b
[해설] https://youtu.be/220mBCWnvaU

158. The local newspaper has an average daily readership of 100,000 people in the region.

[해석] 지역 신문은 이 지역에서 하루 평균 10만 명의 독자층을 보유하고 있다

[어휘] local 지역의 newspaper 신문 average 평균 daily readership 독자층, 독자수 region 지역

[실시간 정답률] https://tinyurl.com/6rdrs4fh
[해설] https://youtu.be/0kl4qszkXmE

159. Our employees demand that the company cafeteria provide a wide variety of food soon.

[해석] 우리 직원들은 회사 식당이 곧 다양한 음식을 제공하기를 요구한다.

[어휘] demand 요구하다 a variety of 다양한 cafeteria 구내 식당

[실시간 정답률] https://tinyurl.com/32wvm647
[해설] https://youtu.be/jEudoGJgssU

160. There is nothing at the present moment that the company can do to restore its reputation.

[해석] 현재 회사가 그 명성을 회복하기 위해 할 수 있는 것은 아무것도 없다.

[어휘] present 현재의 restore 회복하다 reputation 명성

[실시간 정답률] https://tinyurl.com/yretcdmt
[해설] https://youtu.be/lQpdDkB0u7I

해설

161. Our menu offers a wide range of options starting at just $5, so there's something for everyone to enjoy.

[해석] 메뉴는 딱 5달러부터 시작하는 다양한 선택지를 제공해서 모두가 즐길 수 있다.

[어휘] menu 메뉴 offer 제공하다 wide range 다양한 범위 starting at ~부터 시작하는 enjoy 즐기다 just 딱

[실시간 정답률] https://tinyurl.com/5esxe57m
[해설] https://youtu.be/6pDcz60zcXY

162. The Solomon Group has acquired Genova Innovation for an undisclosed amount.

[해석] 솔로몬 그룹은 비공개 금액으로 제노바 이노베이션을 인수했다.

[어휘] acquire 인수하다 for an undisclosed amount 비공개 금액으로

[실시간 정답률] https://tinyurl.com/2h9js5ke
[해설] https://youtu.be/08xVkCw-hSM

163. According to the company regulation, all employees must secure permission before attending external seminars.

[해석] 회사 규정에 따르면 모든 직원은 외부 세미나에 참석하기 전에 허가를 받아야 한다.

[어휘] according to ~에 따르면 company 회사 regulation 규정 secure 확보하다 permission 허가 external 외부의

[실시간 정답률] https://tinyurl.com/3u6jbttd
[해설] https://youtu.be/n3I806rytzk

164. The company had all earnings estimates destroyed due to the threat of regulations.

[해석] 규제 위협으로 인해 회사의 모든 수익 예상치가 파괴되었다.

[어휘] earnings 수익 estimates 예상치 destroyed 파괴된, 붕괴된 threat 위협 regulation 규제

[실시간 정답률] https://tinyurl.com/3xhu7tsf
[해설] https://youtu.be/5M44Qa8WNHw

165. We've just appointed a new marketing assistant, and I am thrilled to have the opportunity to collaborate with someone as skilled and dedicated as Ms. Sato. Let me introduce Mr. Son.

[해석] 우리는 방금 새로운 마케팅 보조를 임명했는데, 저는 사토 씨처럼 숙련되고 헌신적인 사람과 협력할 기회가 생겨 매우 기쁩니다. 손 씨를 소개합니다.

[어휘] appoint 임명하다 marketing 마케팅 assistant 보조 thrilled 기쁜 collaborate 협력하다 skilled 숙련된 dedicated 헌신적인 introduce 소개하다

[실시간 정답률] https://tinyurl.com/y4nz6tbr
[해설] https://youtu.be/SJYy4S99CrQ

166. The tour bus will circle the national park, departing from the main gate every hour on the hour.

[해석] 관광 버스는 매시 정각에 정문에서 출발하여 국립공원을 순환할 것이다.

[어휘] tour bus 관광 버스 circle 순환하다 national park 국립공원 depart 출발하다 main gate 정문

[실시간 정답률] https://tinyurl.com/57npvvfc
[해설] https://youtu.be/F8Ztn0KUFTk

167. Several flower arrangements were sent to the banquet hall before the awards ceremony later this afternoon.

[해석] 이번 오후 늦게 열리는 시상식 전에 몇 가지 꽃 장식이 연회장으로 보내졌다.

[어휘] several 몇 가지 flower arrangements 꽃 장식 send 보내다 banquet hall 연회장 awards ceremony 시상식

[실시간 정답률] https://tinyurl.com/mr4yh76j
[해설] https://youtu.be/JBnih1Duoqs

.

168. Many commuters find rush hour traffic simply unbearable while trying to stay punctual.

[해석] 많은 통근자들은 시간을 지키려고 할 때 러시아워 교통 체증을 단순히 참을 수 없다고 느낀다.

[어휘] commuter 통근자 find 여기다 rush hour traffic 러시아워 교통체증 simply 단순히 unbearable 참을 수 없는 punctual 시간을 지키는

[실시간 정답률] https://tinyurl.com/3j782vak
[해설] https://youtu.be/yG7VeyDJQW8

169. Ms. Jade's passion for helping others succeed has led her to the supporter program.

[해석] 다른 사람들이 성공하도록 돕는 것에 대한 제이드의 열정이 그녀를 지지 프로그램으로 이끌었다.

[어휘] passion 열정 succeed 성공하다
[실시간 정답률] https://tinyurl.com/z4h5bj4c
[해설] https://youtu.be/lmhBSF1SOcM

170. Our hotel boasts 100 guest rooms, most with stunning ocean views.

[해석] 우리 호텔은 멋진 바다 전망을 자랑하는 100개의 객실을 보유하고 있는데, 그 중 대부분이 바다 전망이다.

[어휘] boasts 자랑하다 guest rooms 객실 stunning 멋진, 굉장한 ocean view 바다 전망

[실시간 정답률] https://tinyurl.com/5y7fxv2f
[해설] https://youtu.be/6KfCmNGBAvA

해설

171. Subscribe to our premium luxury watch magazine today and receive one month of trial use.

[해석] 오늘 프리미엄 럭셔리 시계 잡지에 구독하고 한 달간의 무료 사용을 받아보세요.

[어휘] subscribe 구독하다 premium luxury watch magazine 프리미엄 럭셔리 시계 잡지 today 오늘 one month of trial use 한 달간의 무료 사용

[실시간 정답률] https://tinyurl.com/zxj4tpwa
[해설] https://youtu.be/Yl3ymMk5s60

172. With technology advancing rapidly, the company is investing heavily in research and development.

[해석] 기술이 빠르게 발전함에 따라, 회사는 연구 및 개발에 대규모 투자하고 있습니다.

[어휘] technology 기술 advance 발전하다 rapidly 빠르게 invest 투자하다 research and development 연구 및 개발 heavily 대규모로
[실시간 정답률] https://tinyurl.com/yc35zuj5
[해설] https://youtu.be/gkP7w_QQSV0

173. Mr. Han made complaints about the way many patients like himself were treated in the hospital.

[해석] 한 씨는 자신과 같은 많은 환자들이 병원에서 대해지는 방식에 대해 불평을 했다.

[어휘] made 했다 complaints 불평 way 방식 patient 환자 treat 다루다, 대하다, 취급하다, 사주다

[실시간 정답률] https://tinyurl.com/4ddjhnzt
[해설] https://youtu.be/Ov25Orvtdkl

174. Tech Innovations is making strategic changes to align with evolving industry standards.

[해석] 테크 이노베이션은 발전하는 산업 표준에 맞추기 위해 전략적인 변화를 이루고 있습니다.

[어휘] strategic 전략적인 changes 변화 align with ~에 맞추다 evolving 발전하는 industry standard 산업 표준

[실시간 정답률] https://tinyurl.com/yd7fzkye
[해설] https://youtu.be/AKX0djHjClU

175. Those who live in rural areas are overwhelmingly in favor of building a hospital near their town.

[해석] 농촌 지역에 사는 사람들은 대다수가 자신들의 마을 근처에 병원을 짓는 것을 매우 찬성한다.

[어휘] rural 농촌 area 지역 overwhelmingly 압도적으로 in favor of ~를 찬성하여

[실시간 정답률] https://tinyurl.com/ykh32n72
[해설] https://youtu.be/X4kqYgO8-sM

176. To initiate a maintenance request, report the issue with all relevant details through the online system.

[해석] 유지보수 요청을 시작하기 위해, 온라인 시스템을 통해 모든 관련 세부사항과 함께 문제를 보고하라.

[어휘] initiate 시작하다 maintenance 유지보수 relevant 관련된

[실시간 정답률] https://tinyurl.com/2c3uhaex
[해설] https://youtu.be/mbUfCnmWw5Q

177. The Premier Health Insurance package comes with comprehensive dental and vision coverage.

[해석] 프리미어 건강 보험 패키지는 종합적인 치과 및 시력 보장을 포함하고 있다.

[어휘] comprehensive 종합적인 dental 치과 vision 시력 coverage 보장

[실시간 정답률] https://tinyurl.com/3rskcwbh
[해설] https://youtu.be/tEBxd83ea8U

178. If you need support during regular business hours, our after-hours emergency service is available.

[해석] 정규 업무 시간 중 지원이 필요한 경우, 우리의 야간 비상 서비스를 이용할 수 있다.

[어휘] support 지원 regular 정규 business hours 업무 시간 available 이용할 수 있는

[실시간 정답률] https://tinyurl.com/tha33b75
[해설] https://youtu.be/DvY-KnrmL1E

179. Debongi's Grocery clerks are trained to remain attentive to even the demanding needs of some customers.

[해석] 데본지의 식료품점 점원들은 부 고객의 까다로운 요구에도 주의 깊게 대응하도록 훈련받는다.

[어휘] trained 훈련받다 remain 유지하다 attentive 주의 깊은 demanding 까다로운

[실시간 정답률] https://tinyurl.com/2xcscs3c
[해설] https://youtu.be/XG-2-yPNJvo

180. The marketing team needs to determine the target audience for our new product launch.

[해석] 마케팅 팀은 새로운 제품 출시를 위한 목표 고객들을 알아내야 한다.

[어휘] marketing team 마케팅 팀 determine 알아내다 target audience 목표 고객 product launch 제품 출시

[실시간 정답률] https://tinyurl.com/4zreh6t7
[해설] https://youtu.be/eyrLOAY4pqM

해설

181. The replaced laser printer produces up to 30,000 pages per toner cartridge, requiring fewer replacements.

[해석] 교체된 레이저 프린터는 토너 카트리지 당 최대 30,000 페이지를 출력하여 교체품 교환 횟수가 줄어든다.

[어휘] replaced 교체된 laser printer 레이저 프린터 produce 생산하다, 출력하다

[실시간 정답률] https://tinyurl.com/mvv9tkeu
[해설] https://youtu.be/Wddlabm6Q_A

182. Café Delight's commitment to freshness is noticeable across its entire menu of artisanal coffees and homemade pastries.

[해석] 카페 딜라이트의 신선함에 대한 헌신은 그들의 모든 수제 커피와 수제 패스트리 메뉴에서 눈에 띈다.

[어휘] commitment 헌신 freshness 신선함 artisanal 수제의

[실시간 정답률] https://tinyurl.com/mscfwsdx
[해설] https://youtu.be/8ClQJ0utdTg

183. All plants in the greenhouse are protected from high, potentially damaging temperatures.

[해석] 온실의 모든 식물은 잠재적으로 해를 끼칠 수 있는 높은 온도로부터 보호받고 있다.

[어휘] protect 보호하다 potentially 잠재적으로 damaging 해를 끼치는 temperature 온도

[실시간 정답률] https://tinyurl.com/3b97c5tk
[해설] https://youtu.be/0LEbxs0wdNI

184. Despite starting late, Ms. Park completed the task with an exceptionally impressive time.

[해석] 늦게 시작했음에도 불구하고, 박 씨는 대단히 인상적인 시간에 업무를 완료했다.

[어휘] despite ~에도 불구하고 start 시작하다 late 늦게 complete 완료하다 task 업무 exceptionally 대단히 impressive 인상적인

[실시간 정답률] https://tinyurl.com/hvbzubv4
[해설] https://youtu.be/HoAMgVcx0I4?

185. Architect Kim is credited with designing the innovative eco-friendly skyscraper in the city.

[해석] 건축가 김은 도시의 혁신적인 친환경 초고층 빌딩 설계에 공로를 인정받았다.

[어휘] architect 건축가 be credited with 공로를 인정받다 design 설계하다 innovative 혁신적인 eco-friendly 친환경 skyscraper 초고층 빌딩

[실시간 정답률] https://tinyurl.com/bdfc9rms
[해설] https://youtu.be/budmvZ1a-Qc

186. Ms. Uraha's new book explains what it takes to make one's hobby a successful business.

[해석] 우하라 씨의 새로운 책은 한 사람의 취미가 성공적인 사업체가 되기 위해서 무엇이 필요한 지를 설명한다.

[어휘] explain 설명하다, 다루다 what it takes 필요한 것 business 사업체, 회사

[실시간 정답률] https://tinyurl.com/27r72wcp
[해설] https://youtu.be/gYKcbzPaR64

187. The magazine includes an article that analyzes in detail how seriously global warming and air pollution can affect our lives.

[해석] 이 잡지에는 지구 온난화와 공기 오염이 우리의 삶에 얼마나 심각한 영향을 미칠 수 있는지 자세히 분석하는 기사가 실려 있다.

[어휘] analyze 분석하다 in detail 자세히 global warming 지구 온난화 air pollution 공기 오염 affect 영향을 끼치다 live 삶

[실시간 정답률] https://tinyurl.com/4nd5ft2a
[해설] https://youtu.be/Ex2WrZN0wlY

188. Upon receiving the grant proposal, the funding agency will evaluate its merits and decide on the allocation of resources.

[해석] 보조금 제안서를 받은 후 자금 기관은 그의 장점을 평가하고 자원의 할당을 결정할 것이다.

[어휘] upon -ing ~ 하자 마자 receive 받다 grant proposal 보조금 제안서 funding agency 자금 기관 evaluate 평가하다 merit 장점 decide 결정 allocation 할당 resource 자원

[실시간 정답률] https://tinyurl.com/ybd6nxk9
[해설] https://youtu.be/zYqtT1RPYq0

189. The annual festival brings a burst of energy and excitement to every corner of what is otherwise a quiet town.

[해석] 연간 축제는 그렇지 않았더라면 조용한 마을의 모든 구석에 에너지와 흥분을 가져다준다.

[어휘] annual 연간 festival 축제 brings 가져다주다 burst of energy 에너지 폭발 excitement 흥분 every corner 모든 구석 quiet 조용한 town 마을

[실시간 정답률] https://tinyurl.com/3ed8fcxv
[해설] https://youtu.be/pPlAtWlFVc8

190. If your order sustains any damage during shipment, we'll provide a replacement.

[해석] 귀하의 주문이 배송 중에 어떠한 손상을 입으면, 우리는 대체품을 제공할 것입니다.

[어휘] order 주문 sustains 입다 damage 손상 during 중에 shipment 배송 provide 제공하다 replacement 대체품

[실시간 정답률] https://tinyurl.com/mr2hyavk
[해설] https://youtu.be/CbbyaJvSpFM

해설

191. The Riverdale Public Library will be closed for another three weeks during the renovation.

[해석] 리버데 공공 도서관은 리모델링 동안 추가로 세 주 동안 폐쇄될 것이다.

[어휘] closed 폐쇄되다 renovation 리모델링

[실시간 정답률] https://tinyurl.com/ms9jf2a4
[해설] https://youtu.be/2KXJwb1WFF0

192. The stock price per share of Zenith Innovations is projected to comfortably exceed $800 by the end of the month.

[해석] 제니스 이노베이션즈의 주당 주가는 이달 말까지 편안하게 800달러를 초과할 것으로 예상된다.

[어휘] stock price 주가 per share 주당 project 예상하다 comfortably 편안하게 exceed 초과하다

[실시간 정답률] https://tinyurl.com/w7dr73kf
[해설] https://youtu.be/vsrrUYd2lyc

193. Zenith Innovations has expanded its customer bases in several new countries.

[해석] 제니스 이노베이션은 여러 신규 국가에서 고객 기반을 확장했다.

[어휘] expand 확장하다 customer base 고객 기반 several 여러 new country 신규 국가

[실시간 정답률] https://tinyurl.com/ym77a4d3
[해설] https://youtu.be/fy9T4iTfSv4

194. The amount of money invested in the venture is deemed to be considerable enough to affect the local economy.

[해석] 이 벤처에 투자된 돈의 양은 지역 경제에 영향을 줄 만큼 상당하다고 여겨진다.

[어휘] amount of money 돈의 양 invested 투자된 venture 벤처 deemed 여겨진 considerable 상당한 affect 영향을 주다 local economy 지역 경제

[실시간 정답률] https://tinyurl.com/4peduk44
[해설] https://youtu.be/WgWvxdl7PBM

195. Riverdale Electronics operates three branch locations in the Greater Los Angeles area to better serve our regional clients.

[해석] Riverdale Electronics는 로스앤젤레스 대도시 지역의 고객들에게 더 나은 서비스를 제공하기 위해 세 개의 지점을 운영합니다.

[어휘] operates 운영하다 locations 지점들

[실시간 정답률] https://tinyurl.com/2hz3tek4
[해설] https://youtu.be/nS_INVsAe68

196. A broader selection of genres at the city park's musical performance was offered compared to other concerts in the area.

[해석] 도시 공원의 음악 공연에서는 지역의 다른 콘서트와 비교하여 보다 넓은 다양한 장르들이 제공되었다.

[어휘] broader 더 넓은 genres 장르 musical performance 음악 공연 compared to 비교하여 other 다른

[실시간 정답률] https://tinyurl.com/3pz252c2
[해설] https://youtu.be/jDpQWpgcJSw

197. The theater had to make program adjustments due to the new performance schedule.

[해석] 극장은 새로운 공연 정으로 인해 프로그램을 조정해야 했습니다.

[어휘] theater 극장 program adjustments 프로그램 조정 due to ~때문에 new performance schedule 새로운 공연 정

[실시간 정답률] https://tinyurl.com/2jdmwm3h
[해설] https://youtu.be/F2RaSoIraUU

198. We will issue a new ID card that provides access to the laboratory as per your request.

[해석] 우리는 당신의 요청에 따라 연구실에 접근할 수 있는 새로운 신분증을 발급할 것입니다.

[어휘] issue 발급하다 new 새로운 ID card 신분증 provide 제공하다 access 접근 laboratory 연구실 per 따라 request 요청

[실시간 정답률] https://tinyurl.com/3dhnn4cx
[해설] https://youtu.be/TviN6mYUZGU

199. Seminar participants carefully examining what others do in their group help finish collaborative work quickly.

[해석] 세미나 참가자들은 그룹에서 다른 사람들이 하는 을 주의 깊게 살피면서 협업 작업을 빨리 끝내는 데 도움을 준다.

[어휘] participant 참가자 carefully 주의 깊게 examine 살피다 collaborative work 협업 작업

[실시간 정답률] https://tinyurl.com/8xr3uxfs
[해설] https://youtu.be/LuMqzvjdBNw

200. The members of the waitstaff were trained to serve additional portions of side dishes only if they were requested.

[해석] 웨이터스태프 구성원들은 요청이 있을 때만 추가 반찬을 제공하도록 훈련되었다.

[어휘] waitstaff 식당 종업원 trained 훈련된 serve 제공하다 additional 추가적인 portion 1인분 side dishe 반찬 requested 요청된

[실시간 정답률] https://tinyurl.com/469x2kxx
[해설] https://youtu.be/nAer7yp1QaQ

해설

201. Launching the new product proved to be quite the experience for Electro Solutions.

[해석] 새 제품을 출시하는 것은 Electro Solutions에게 상당한 경험이 되는 이었다.

[어휘] experienced 경험이 많은
[실시간 정답률] https://tinyurl.com/32457aae
[해설] https://youtu.be/Rl2Argi2IZM

202. We will inform you whcih design proposal we will select later this week.

[해석] 우리는 이번 주 후반경에 어떤 디자인 제안을 선택할 지를 알려줄 것이다.

[어휘] inform 알려주다 design proposal 디자인 제안 select 선택하다 later this week 이번 주 후반경에

[실시간 정답률] https://tinyurl.com/2nuda6bu
[해설] https://youtu.be/P0wvcky65bE

203. This year's Literary Award will be awarded to Jonathan Parker, the lead author of the recently published novel 'Echoes of Eternity.' He is to be recognized during a ceremony at the Grand Theater on Sunday, May 5.

[해석] 올해의 문학상은 최근에 출판된 'Echoes of Eternity'의 주요 저자인 Jonathan Parker에게 수여될 예정이다. 그는 5월 5 요 그랜드 극장에서 열리는 시상식에서 상을 받을 예정이다.

[어휘] award 수여하다 recognized 치하하다, 상주다 ceremony 시상식

[실시간 정답률] https://tinyurl.com/mpm47w3x
[해설] https://youtu.be/tvYCbD-N1Ng

204. Mr. Samson received an award for his creative incorporation of new ideas into a business plan.

[해석] 샘슨 씨는 새로운 아이디어를 사업 계획에 창의적으로 통합한 것에 대해 상을 받았다.

[어휘] creative 창의적인 incorporation 통합 business plan 사업 계획

[실시간 정답률] https://tinyurl.com/d8smnedy
[해설] https://youtu.be/0WWrexsKhME

205. Mr. Park opted to pay for the furniture by installments over a period of six months.

[해석] 박 씨는 가구를 6개월 동안 분납으로 지불하기로 결정했다.

[어휘] opt to ~하기로 결정하다 pay 지불하다 furniture 가구 installments 분납 period 기간

[실시간 정답률] https://tinyurl.com/yf7rb8p8
[해설] https://youtu.be/9wLNRj6jOyk

206. Honeyville and Pleasantville are becoming two of the fastest-growing towns in the province.

[해석] 허니빌과 플레전트빌은 이 지방에서 가장 빠르게 성장하는 두 도시가 되고 있다.

[어휘] become 되다 fastest-growing 가장 빠르게 성장하는 province 지방

[실시간 정답률] https://tinyurl.com/mc5cskeb
[해설] https://youtu.be/UlCQ45Z327w

207. Employees at T&C cannot take more than one week of paid vacation pending approval by the board of directors.

[해석] T&C의 직원들은 이사회의 승인을 기다리는 동안, 유급 휴가를 1주 이상 사용할 수 없다.

[어휘] employees 직원 paid vacation 유급 휴가 approve 승인하다 board of directors 이사회

[실시간 정답률] https://tinyurl.com/bdede5rf
[해설] https://youtu.be/VJPni5ycix4

208. After the concert, Ms. Smith searched for a limited-edition shirt, but there were none available.

[해석] 콘서트가 끝난 후, 스미스 씨는 한정판 셔츠를 찾았지만 사용할 수 있는 것이 하나도 없었다.

[어휘] after 후 concert 콘서트 searched 찾다 limited-edition 한정판 shirt 셔츠 none 하나도 없는 available 사용할 수 있는

[실시간 정답률] https://tinyurl.com/5fpfphk4
[해설] https://youtu.be/bQpy6z8k_Ck

209. A large amount of Chinese capital is being directed toward acquiring a new entertainment venture.

[해석] 많은 중국 자본이 새로운 엔터테인먼트 사업을 인수하기 위해 할당되고 있다.

[어휘] capital 자본 direct 보내다, 할당하다 acquire 인수하다 venture 벤쳐사업

[실시간 정답률] https://tinyurl.com/bdeukt3z
[해설] https://youtu.be/y78Xj9soPVU

210. Evergreen Hiking supplies the finest outdoor equipment and clothing around.

[해석] 에버그린 하이킹은 현존하는 가장 뛰어난 아웃도어 장비와 의류를 공급한다.

[어휘] supplies 공급하다 finest 가장 뛰어난 outdoor 아웃도어 equipment 장비 clothing 의류

[실시간 정답률] https://tinyurl.com/mvchbbv
[해설] https://youtu.be/X-KmY5yjy9w

해설

211. Even if you opt to cancel your subscription, no further action is needed.

[해석] 구독을 취소하기로 선택하더라도 추가 조치는 필요하지 않습니다.

[어휘] Even if ~하더라도 opt 선택하다 cancel 취소하다 subscription 구독 further 추가의 action 조치 needed 필요한

[실시간 정답률] https://tinyurl.com/2n979229
[해설] https://youtu.be/IEjhDBg1n3o

212. All sales are final during our clearance event, so choose wisely.

[해석] 저희 청소 이벤트 동안 모든 판매는 최종적이므로 신중하게 선택하십시오.

[어휘] sales are final 교환/환불이 안되다 clearance 재고 정리

[실시간 정답률] https://tinyurl.com/kbueasfw
[해설] https://youtu.be/JGaRzHi3c1s

213. The newly appointed project manager is open to feedback from her team members.

[해석] 새로 임명된 프로젝트 매니저는 팀원들의 피드백에 개방적이다.

[어휘] appointed 임명된 be open to ~에 개방적인 feedback 피드백

[실시간 정답률] https://tinyurl.com/5f79wcef
[해설] https://youtu.be/9zmdz1R9zjw

214. Due to the construction work on 5th Avenue next week, there should be minor delays.

[해석] 다음 주 5번가의 건설 작업으로 인해 약간의 지연이 있을 것이다.

[어휘] construction 건설 work 작업 delays 지연

[실시간 정답률] https://tinyurl.com/y4ja5j4a
[해설] https://youtu.be/k2w0pT0bguA

215. In light of the severe weather forecast, the company is implementing a remote working policy.

[해석] 심각한 날씨 예보를 고려하여 회사는 원격 근무 정책을 시행하고 있다.

[어휘] In light of ~을 고려하여 severe 심각한 weather forecast 날씨 예보 implement 시행하다 remote working 원격 근무 policy 정책

[실시간 정답률] https://tinyurl.com/2v8u5zfe
[해설] https://youtu.be/aHSeTLiu17U

216. London Logistics cut its incidental expenses by laying off its administrative workforce in addition to closing several local offices.

[해석] 런던 로지스틱스는 여러 지역 사무소를 닫는 것 외에도 행정 인력을 감축함으로써 부대 비용을 절감했다.

[어휘] cut 감축하다 incidental expenses 부대 비용 administrative workforce 행정 인력 in addition to ~외에도 closing 닫는 것 several 여러 local office 지역 사무소

[실시간 정답률] https://tinyurl.com/ymve9dbh
[해설] https://youtu.be/W6aexpSW-5U

217. Innovative technologies are enabling businesses to reach markets they might not otherwise have accessed.

[해석] 혁신적인 기술은 기업들이 그들이 접근하지 않았을 것 같은 시장에 접근할 수 있도록 해주고 있다.

[어휘] innovative 혁신적인 technologies 기술들 enable 가능하게 하다 businesses 기업들 reach 도달하다 otherwise 그렇지 않았더라면 access 접근하다

[실시간 정답률] https://tinyurl.com/34tcs8dv
[해설] https://youtu.be/1lRrxVnOSNw

218. Zephyr Innovations will invest in its facility expansion to increase production capacity and meet growing demand.

[해석] Zephyr Innovations는 생산 능력을 늘리고 증가하는 수요를 충족시키기 위해 시설 확장에 투자할 것이다.

[어휘] invest 투자하다 expansion 확장 production capacity 생산 능력 demand 수요

[실시간 정답률] https://tinyurl.com/36p6z7zx
[해설] https://youtu.be/skV2-Ux-vL4

219. No unauthorized personnel are allowed to access the secure data center.

[해석] 인가되지 않은 인원들은 아무도 보안 데이터 센터에 접근하도록 허락되지 않습니다.

[어휘] unauthorized 인가되지 않은 personnel 인원 allowed 허용된 access 접근 secure 보안의, 안전한

[실시간 정답률] https://tinyurl.com/a3nr9h99
[해설] https://youtu.be/VkKq9v-NNMo

220. Providing feedback on a coworker could be uncomfortable, especially if there is critisim involved.

[해석] 동료에게 피드백을 주는 것은 불편할 수 있고 특히 비판이 개입되면 더하다.

[어휘] feedback 피드백 coworker 동료 uncomfortable 불편한 criticism 비판 involved 개입된, 연루된

[실시간 정답률] https://tinyurl.com/bdcrj4t3
[해설] https://youtu.be/k_on8ZuJpw0

해설

221. Goldcable provides a direct withdrawal program that subscribers can apply to without complicated documentation.

[해석] 골드케이블은 복잡한 서류 없이 가입자가 신청할 수 있는 직접 출금 프로그램을 제공합니다.

[어휘] provide 제공하다 direct 직접적인 withdrawal program 출금 프로그램 subscriber 가입자 apply to ~에 가입하다 without ~없이 complicated 복잡한 documentation 서류

[실시간 정답률] https://tinyurl.com/drzp24ue
[해설] https://youtu.be/6s7sIMshvFM

222. One of our technicians will visit your facility to assess the breakage that resulted from misuse.

[해석] 우리 기술자 중 한 명이 남용으로 인한 파손을 평가하기 위해 시설을 방문할 것이다.

[어휘] technician 기술자 assess 평가하다 breakage 파손 misuse 남용

[실시간 정답률] https://tinyurl.com/efvx2p5b
[해설] https://youtu.be/F1Daqpj-JNc

223. Our menu features items from Lily's Confectionery, a neighborhood gem for years.

[해석] 우리 메뉴는 수년 동안 지역 사람들에게 사랑받는 릴리 제과점의 제품들을 특징으로 한다.

[어휘] menu 메뉴 features 특징으로 하다 items 제품들 neighborhood 지역의 gem 보석, 여기서는 '인기 장소'

[실시간 정답률] https://tinyurl.com/bzpea764
[해설] https://youtu.be/86GYVYgH1yc

224. Farmers in Punjab offer fresh produce to local schools at a fraction of market prices.

[해석] 펀자브의 농부들은 시장 가격의 아주 적은 부분에 해당하는 금액으로 현지 학교에 신선한 농산물을 제공한다.

[어휘] farmer 농부 offer 제공하다 fresh 신선한 produce 농산물

[실시간 정답률] https://tinyurl.com/4rbw55sn
[해설] https://youtu.be/ynvylpILqv8

225. The product you ordered from our online shop is unavailable until June 1.

[해석] 당신이 온라인 쇼핑몰에서 주문한 제품은 6월 1까지는 재고가 없을 것입니다.

[어휘] product 제품 order 주문하다 online shop 온라인 쇼핑몰 unavailable 이용 불가능한 until ~까지 June 1 6월 1

[실시간 정답률] https://tinyurl.com/ypbvdynx
[해설] https://youtu.be/ozm8ib7jOi0

226. Sales at Baxter Plaza reportedly dropped when a rival superstore opened just a block away.

[해석] 들리는 바에 따르면, 경쟁 슈퍼스토어가 바로 한 블록 떨어진 곳에 개장했을 때, 배스터 플라자의 매출이 감소했다고 한다.

[어휘] sales 매출 reportedly 들리는 바에 따르면 drop 감소하다 rival 경쟁의 open 개장하다 away 떨어진

[실시간 정답률] https://tinyurl.com/9krbwcy6
[해설] https://youtu.be/aQs8YtEfU2s

227. The new highway reduced the travel time from Los Angeles to San Francisco by 2 hours.

[해석] 새로운 고속도로는 로스앤젤레스에서 샌프란시스코까지의 이동 시간을 2시간 단축시켰다.

[어휘] reduce 단축시키다 travel time 이동 시간

[실시간 정답률] https://tinyurl.com/4e4febmc
[해설] https://youtu.be/YC2uSrpnw-k

228. The manager is praised for being patient with her team members and customers alike.

[해석] 매니저는 팀원과 고객 모두에게 인내심이 있게 대한다고 칭찬을 받는다.

[어휘] praise 칭찬하다 be patient with ~에게 인내심 있게 대하다 A and B alike A와 B 둘다

[실시간 정답률] https://tinyurl.com/yhkc7jxt
[해설] https://youtu.be/iGOtD9UunTc

229. Apply diligence to ensure all client communications are clear and detailed.

[해석] 모든 고객과의 의사소통이 명확하고 상세하게 되도록 신중히 하세요.

[어휘] apply diligence 신중히 하다 ensure 보장하다 client 고객 communications 의사소통 clear 명확한 detailed 상세한

[실시간 정답률] https://tinyurl.com/mr2n4ykb
[해설] https://youtu.be/6FpfLYtzlfl

230. Recognized as the trendsetter and industry standard, Oleo is the definitive domestic wine producer in the nation.

[해석] 트렌드 세터이자 업계 표준으로 인정받는 올레오는 국내에서 최고의 와인 생산자입니다.

[어휘] recognized 인정받는 trendsetter 트렌드 세터 industry 업계 standard 표준 definitive 최고의 domestic 국내의 wine producer 와인 생산자

[실시간 정답률] https://tinyurl.com/2p9udkjr
[해설] https://youtu.be/Foe8_TD27qs

해설

231. On top of a wide playground, the park will also feature a fully accessible multi-purpose field.

[해석] 넓은 놀이터뿐만 아니라, 이 공원은 완전히 접근 가능한 다목적 필드도 갖추게 될 것이다.

[어휘] wide 넓은 playground 놀이터 feature 특징으로 하다 fully 완전히 accessible 접근 가능한 multi-purpose 다목적 field 필드

[실시간 정답률] https://tinyurl.com/4rn5ddja
[해설] https://youtu.be/UvYXD2xK7qw

232. The promotional offer from Quick Deal Store is only good until the end of this week.

[해석] 퀵딜 스토어가 제공하는 프로모션 제공은 이번 주 마지막까지만 유효하다.

[어휘] promotional offer 프로모션 제공 provide 제공하다 good 유효한 only until ~까지 end 마지막 week 주

[실시간 정답률] https://tinyurl.com/mr3kyxbk
[해설] https://youtu.be/XctAvjtwElA

233. We didn't have enough time during the meeting to discuss the budget deficit.

[해석] 예산 적자에 대해 논의할 충분한 시간이 회의 중에 없었다.

[어휘] enough 충분한 time 시간 discuss 논의하다 budget deficit 예산 적자 meeting 회의 during ~동안에

[실시간 정답률] https://tinyurl.com/8wn6f922
[해설] https://youtu.be/FvZOauFu4-4

234. The book *Ad Innovate*, said to be a key resource in digital advertising, has revolutionized modern marketing approaches.

[해석] 디지털 광고의 핵심 자원으로 언급되는 'Ad Innovate'라는 책은 현대 마케팅 접근법을 혁신적으로 변화시켰다.

[어휘] key resource 핵심 자원 digital 디지털 advertising 광고 revolutionize 혁신적으로 변화시키다 modern 현대의 approaches 접근법

[실시간 정답률] https://tinyurl.com/mvwm3rcu
[해설] https://youtu.be/aqrSdbfuXvA

235. During our tour, we encountered a lot of traffic, which caused some delays. However, the highlight was our guide, who was excellent at bringing the history of each place to life with fascinating stories. The last thing I wanted was to rush through any of the stops without fully hearing the stories behind them.

[해석] 우리 투어 중에 교통 체증을 많이 만났고, 이로 인해 몇 가지 지연이 발생했다. 그러나 이번 투어의 하이라이트는 각 장소의 역사를 흥미로운 이야기로 생생하게 전달해 준 우리 가이드였다. 나는 그 장소들의 이야기를 제대로 듣지 못하고 서둘러 지나치는 것을 절대 원하지 않았다.

[어휘] tour 투어 encounter 직면하다 cause 야기하다 delays 지연 highlight 하이라이트 guide 가이드 excellent 탁월한 bringing to life 생생하게 만들다 rush 서두르다 stops 정류장

[실시간 정답률] https://tinyurl.com/25fkne4h
[해설] https://youtu.be/p2hl70xQVPE

236. Sebatonic Chemicals, Inc. announced today it has successfully developed a new variety of strawberries that resist rising temperatures.

[해석] 세바토닉 화학 주식회사는 오늘 상승하는 온도에 저항하는 새로운 종류의 딸기를 성공적으로 개발했다고 발표했다.

[어휘] announce 발표하다 successfully 성공적으로 develope 개발하다 resist 저항하다 temperature 온도

[실시간 정답률] https://tinyurl.com/3kkyd2bn
[해설] https://youtu.be/JXI2jQBMr8s

237. Many thanks to Rebecca Lin for the remarkable work on the Orion account.

[해석] 오리온 계정에 대한 뛰어난 작업에 대해 리베카 린에게 많은 감사를 드립니다.

[어휘] Many thanks to 감사를 드립니다 remarkable 뛰어난 work 작업 account 계정

[실시간 정답률] https://tinyurl.com/4f629442
[해설] https://youtu.be/bL0b0lFYpZ8

238. Ian Macdonald is among the top ten musicians in America, behind only the Western Boys in album sales.

[해석] Ian Macdonald는 미국에서 상위 10명의 음악가 중 한 명이며, 앨범 판매에서 오직 Western Boys 뒤에 있다.

[어휘] among ~중에서 top ten 상위 10명 musicians 음악가들 behind ~뒤에 album sales 앨범 판매

[실시간 정답률] https://tinyurl.com/ye23vxtn
[해설] https://youtu.be/x2Qe1Y_yb5E

239. The contractor was unhappy when the potential employer did not select either of the proposals.

[해석] 도급업체는 잠재적 고용주가 제안된 두 가지 안 중 어느 것도 선택하지 않았을 때 불만족스러웠다.

[어휘] contractor 도급업체, 하청업체 potential 잠재적인 employer 고용주 select 선택하다 proposal 제안

[실시간 정답률] https://tinyurl.com/2n6dbbcv
[해설] https://youtu.be/D3wJU8XTwOQ

240. Once the most popular structure in town, Sumatra Pagoda has been rarely visited in recent years.

[해석] 한때 마을에서 가장 인기 있는 구조물이었던 수마트라 파고다는 최근 몇 년 동안 드물게 방문되었다.

[어휘] once 한때 popular 인기 있는 structure 구조물 rarely 드물게 visit 방문하다

[실시간 정답률] https://tinyurl.com/35dj74sv
[해설] https://youtu.be/hYWHclOj7cU

해설

241. Mr. Wright wanted to alert his coworker to some business opportunity.

[해석] 라이트 씨는 동료에게 어떤 사업 기회에 대해 알리고 싶어했다.

[어휘] inform 알리다 alert 경보를 발하다, 알리다, 기민한 coworker 동료 business opportunity 사업 기회

[실시간 정답률] https://tinyurl.com/4fw2htj9
[해설] https://youtu.be/sZUR4jZiXso

242. Celestial Movements is the fourth most widely broadcast documentary series in prime time.

[해석] 셀레스티얼 무브먼츠는 프라임 타임에서 가장 널리 방송되는 네 번째 다큐멘터리 시리즈입니다.

[어휘] fourth 네 번째 widely 널리 broadcast 방송되는 documentary 시리즈 prime time 프라임 타임

[실시간 정답률] https://tinyurl.com/4hey8cnj
[해설] https://youtu.be/NYtyqzeraHU

243. The renovation work will extend past Thursday if the weather becomes an issue.

[해석] 날씨가 문제가 될 경우 리모델링 작업이 목요 이후로 연장될 것이다.

[어휘] renovation work 리모델링 작업 extend 연장되다 past Thursday 목요 이후 weather 날씨 become an issue 문제가 되다

[실시간 정답률] https://tinyurl.com/b3vz46w7
[해설] https://youtu.be/GbxRCLY-5Jg

244. Sal's Ristorante Italiano, said to be the most popular restaurant in town, provides authentic Italian cuisine.

[해석] 살스 리스토란테 이탈리아노는 마을에서 가장 인기 있는 레스토랑으로 여겨지며, 정통 이탈리아 요리를 제공한다.

[어휘] most popular 가장 인기 있는 restaurant 레스토랑 town 마을 provides 제공한다 authentic 정통 Italian cuisine 이탈리아 요리

[실시간 정답률] https://tinyurl.com/yxtft7yf
[해설] https://youtu.be/VJ45_ezDL6o

245. It's easy for you to purchase additional coverage ----- the manufacturer's warranty.

[해석] 제조사의 보증에 추가 보증을 구입하는 것이 쉽다.

[어휘] additional 추가적인 coverage 보상 warranty 보증

[실시간 정답률] https://tinyurl.com/3u9kvy74
[해설] https://youtu.be/NzVnXUb167Q

246. Text Santonio Tech Support to receive immediate assistance with technical issues.

[해석] 산토니오 기술 지원에 문자를 보내 즉각적인 기술 지원을 받으십시오.

[어휘] text 문자를 보내다 Santonio Tech Support 산토니오기술 지원 receive 받다 immediate 즉각적인 assistance 지원 technical issues 기술적 문제

[실시간 정답률] https://tinyurl.com/3s9ef33e
[해설] https://youtu.be/0gz6kemyqVk

247. With no laptops at their disposal, most of the students in Peaceville were unable to attend online classes.

[해석] 노트북이 없는 학생들은 대부분 온라인 수업에 참여할 수 없었다.

[어휘] disposal 사용할 수 있음 unable 불가능한 attend 참여하다 online classes 온라인 수업

[실시간 정답률] https://tinyurl.com/2vjvxhh5
[해설] https://youtu.be/eKlHdpz4WTM

248. Mr. Smith realized the moment he read the proposal it was a game-changer for his startup.

[해석] 스미스 씨는 제안서를 읽는 순간 그것이 자신의 스타트업에 게임 체인저가 될 것임을 깨달았다.

[어휘] realize 깨닫다 the moment 딱 ~한 순간 read 읽다 proposal 제안서 game-changer 게임 체인저 startup 스타트업

[실시간 정답률] https://tinyurl.com/3kaet83b
[해설] https://youtu.be/cd9Gvlz_FBM

249. The new product was completely sold out just a few hours into the morning.

[해석] 새 제품은 오전 몇 시간 만에 완판되었다.

[어휘] sold out 완판된 just a few hours into the morning 아침에 몇시간 안되어

[실시간 정답률] https://tinyurl.com/38zwyhmu
[해설] https://youtu.be/rmWc19eDQoE

250. The community center is formally hosting a series of workshops on sustainable living.

[해석] 커뮤니티 센터는 지속 가능한 생활에 관한 일련의 워크숍을 공식적으로 개최하고 있다.

[어휘] community center 커뮤니티 센터 host 개최하다 a series of 련의 sustainable 지속 가능한 living 생활

[실시간 정답률] https://tinyurl.com/km6bsfdk
[해설] https://youtu.be/rDykanKz78c